Advance Praise for *God Goes to Work*

"In *God Goes to Work*, Tom helps us to see what is already inside us and what has guided successful businesses through the ages. The way he illuminates spirituality will surprise you. This is a must-read for all business leaders who want to bring their organizations to a new level of trust and openness, productivity, and creativity."

—Sam Yau
Chairman of Esalen Institute

"Tom Zender's *God Goes to Work* is an impassioned vision of unifying business, spirit, prayer, play, and profit. Tom teaches us how to bring God's presence in to our work and business relationships by engaging in 'Spiritual Transactions' that elevate and inspire all involved. Readers will return to work with a new sense of the transformative possibilities of their jobs."

—Rabbi Alan Lurie
Managing Director, Grubb & Ellis, and author of
*Five Minutes on Mondays: Finding Unexpected Purpose,
Peace, and Fulfillment at Work*

"The World Business Academy conducted its first seminar on Spirituality in Business at the Stanford Research Institute's International Hall in 1986. From that day to this, we have been engaged in an on-going inquiry into the nature of spirituality and the implications of its existence as a meta frame or macro lens for business. Tom Zender's book *God Goes to Work* is the most recent eloquent addition to that analysis. It bears the twin marks of great exposition of essential truth, combined with practical wisdom on how to apply the awareness of that essential truth to the workplace."

—Rinaldo S. Brutoco
Founder, President, and CEO
of The World Business Academy

GOD
GOES TO
WORK

GOD GOES TO WORK

NEW THOUGHT PATHS TO PROSPERITY AND PROFITS

TOM ZENDER

with James Cummins

John Wiley & Sons, Inc.

Published by John Wiley & Sons, Inc., Hoboken, New Jersey.
Published simultaneously in Canada.

For general information on our other products and services or for technical support, please contact our Customer Care Department within the United States at (800) 762-2974, outside the United States at (317) 572-3993 or fax (317) 572-4002.

Wiley also publishes its books in a variety of electronic formats. Some content that appears in print may not be available in electronic books. For more information about Wiley products, visit our web site at www.wiley.com.

Library of Congress Cataloging-in-Publication Data:

Zender, Tom, 1939–
    God goes to work: new thought paths to prosperity and profits/Tom Zender, with James Cummins.
        p. cm.
    Includes bibliographical references and index.
    ISBN 978-0-470-56365-6 (cloth)
    e-ISBNs: 978-0-470-61675-8, 978-0-470-61769-4, 978-0-470-61770-0
1. Business–Religious aspects. 2. Management–Religious aspects. I. Cummins, James, 1981–
II. Title.
HF5388.Z46 2010
201'.66584–dc22   2009047254

Printed in the United States of America

10 9 8 7 6 5 4 3 2 1

God Goes to Work *is written in recognition of all working people everywhere in corporations, businesses, and organizations of all sizes and types—for profit, public, private, and nonprofit. It is dedicated to those individuals, managers, executives, leaders, and board members who embrace spirituality in business with the thoughts, words, and actions that raise our collective consciousness to co-create a better world through:*

Business integrity
Conscious commerce
Economic peace

As part of this dedication, I am giving 1 percent of my net proceeds from the sale of this book to global humanitarian causes through registered 501(c)(3) nonprofit organizations.

CONTENTS

FOREWORD

God Goes to Work invokes many of the great universal spiritual principles that I believe are essential to the prosperity of any person or organization. Tom's work here reflects many of the same observations that I have found are the building blocks of health and success.

I have written about how the discovery of quantum physics has led the world into a place where many of the old paradigms no longer fit. In fact, many of these old paradigms are actually making us very sick. Tom captures the heart of this idea in his book by showing how the way in which business has been done over the last century is consistent with a paradigm that is sorely out of date—something based on the physics of Newton and an obsolete understanding of the world around us. By placing modern business in the context of spiritual and quantum rules, Tom has created a model that can help everyone from the CEO to the mail room clerk in their pursuit of a more effective, longer lasting, and more prosperous career. Tom's work goes a long way to help decipher a new way of ending the "tyranny of stress" in business and the economy.

God Goes to Work also demonstrates the value of bringing more peace into our business world—something I have long advocated. Tom's understanding of both spirituality and business has led him to the knowledge that the two are not separate entities—they are two sides of the same coin, and he deftly shows their integration in this timely book. I believe that this way of looking at business and the economy can allow the unlimited potential of peace to enter into the sphere of the corporate world. The results of this are exponential both for the businesses that adhere to these age-old—but new to us—practices and the world around them. This is an exciting idea. Shifting business from old, less useful paradigms toward one that is in tune with the spiritual and physical laws of the universe will no doubt help you and your organization achieve far more for yourselves—and for the world.

—Deepak Chopra
Author, *The Third Jesus:*
The Christ We Cannot Ignore

PREFACE

Just as advanced research is radically altering the way we look at the natural world and what is possible technologically, so, too, must our organizational and management techniques evolve. Advanced research has revealed that our awareness of positive business techniques is radically altering our perception of how taboo issues like spirituality and quantum ideas relate to business. In order to compete in the globalized economy, all people must function at their full potential. But that is not possible if you are subject to a high-stress, inflexible environment, and disconnected expectations.

For centuries, business practices have revolved around an understanding of organizational success that envisions the perfect business as an analog of a perfect machine. The ideas of Isaac Newton, revolutionary during his time, became the template for corporate structuring. Yet it has been a hundred years since the ideas of Newton were replaced in the scientific community, where the founding principles of how to build and maintain a company were shown to be incorrect.

Current successful companies and individuals have begun to instead design their organizations around the principles of quantum physics and relativity. This change has given rise to the "quantum executive": a highly motivating and connected individual whose twin goals—improving his business's profit margins as well as the lives of his colleagues—fully support one another.

The quantum executive is able to do this because he has tapped into an age-old process that has governed the principles of a good business deal since the very beginning—the Spiritual Transactions. A Spiritual Transaction maximizes the potential of every business deal, and is the foundation of the kind of company that can compete in the new economy. These transactions foster a positive atmosphere that allows its members to work harder, faster, and with increased innovation.

I have worked in the information technology industry for decades—both as an innovative engineer and senior executive—but no position affected me as much as my term as president and CEO of Unity. As leader of a faith-based organization that serves more than 3 million people, I have seen the power that spirituality can have when it is used properly in business. As an asset, it is second to none; yet the grand majority of companies are not utilizing it to its full potential.

This book's revelations exhibit the power of the Spiritual Transaction, and demonstrate how to create a quantum business environment that will elevate any company's performance. The basis of all of this, however, comes from the individual—you. You are the only one who can access your full capability and elevate the work of all those around you. Using simple steps and some basic ideas, you will lead a healthier, happier life filled with greater successes than you could have ever imagined for yourself before you discovered the secrets behind the world's most effective transactions.

The ideas in this book show you how to simplify and maximize the quality of your life and organizations to which you belong. The ideas provide the guidelines necessary to excel in a twenty-first-century economy, and to relinquish the unnecessary stress and anxieties so commonly associated with the business world. This is a new way of thinking about business; a New Thought perspective on how to succeed without having that first heart attack at the age of 40. While other books create a complicated set of rules meant to delimit your attention and streamline your efforts, this book helps you expand your attention through simpler and more effective professional practices. It all starts with the realization that you can become a bigger part of the world, and that the world can never get bigger without you.

ACKNOWLEDGMENTS

This book travels a path that moves through the decades of my working life. In this journey, I have had the grateful privilege and honor of being taught, guided, mentored, and uplifted in my business and spiritual passages by so many loving people. To everyone mentioned in the pages of this book, and the thousands who are not, I express my deepest, heartfelt gratitude.

There are those, too, who have been particularly supportive in the development of this book. I give my sincere appreciation:

- To Ken Fisher, my longtime mentor at General Electric and Honeywell, who grounded me in good business practices at the beginning of my career.
- To Dave Hahn, my leader at ITT, who taught me the value of corporate responsibility for the community.
- To the Forum for Corporate Directors, with whom I worked, and who have long recognized and rewarded integrity in the boardroom.
- To Dr. Fred Zook and Dr. Cal Milan, who were my academic advocates and who taught me the significance of spiritually motivated values in business.
- To Dr. Marj Britt, my spiritual mentor for many years, for guiding me in the way of Spirit.
- To all those associated with Unity and the New Thought movement for their loving energy.
- To the people of all faiths everywhere who embrace spirituality in their work.
- To my colleagues and friends with the Association for Global New Thought and the Evolutionary Leaders, who have encouraged me to write and speak to spirituality in business

as a foundation to the conscious evolution of humanity for a better world.

- To my many friends who encouraged me along my path toward this book.

- To James Cummins, a masterful writer, for his unshakable excellence in writing this book with me, and to his mother, Wanda, who led me to him in a moment of divine synchronicity.

- To my agent, Gina Panettieri of Talcott Notch Literary Services for her belief in me, this book, and its purpose.

- To my senior editor and his staff at John Wiley & Sons, Inc., Richard Narramore, for being an example of what this book is about, in expertly and gently guiding me through the editing and publishing process.

- To my wife Wendy and my children Matt and Tommi, and other family members for their unending interest, care, and loving support while I worked on this manuscript.

- To a loving God who cared for me every day of my life—including all workdays!

ABOUT THE AUTHOR

Tom Zender is the President Emeritus of Unity, a transdenominational spiritual movement. Under his leadership from 2001 to 2007, Unity expanded to serve more than 3 million people and members worldwide. He has also held management positions at General Electric, Honeywell, and ITT, and has been senior vice president of three publicly held corporations. In addition to his experience with large corporations, he has served in several smaller and start-up companies as an interim executive, often as CEO.

Tom has been on numerous corporate boards, including those of NASDAQ, Toronto Stock Exchange, as well as companies listed on other exchanges. His nonprofit board positions have included Ottawa University and the Forum for Corporate Directors. He currently is on the nonprofit boards of the Association for Global New Thought and the Evolutionary Leaders for the conscious evolution of a greater humanity.

Tom is a sought after speaker when it comes to the topic of spirituality in business, raising corporate consciousness for business integrity, conscious commerce, and economic peace. He currently lives in Irvine, California, and is married to Wendy Zender Ph.D.

GOD
GOES TO
WORK

1

LEARN THE SECRETS OF THE NEW ECONOMY, ENSURE YOUR PLACE AT THE TOP

Willingness to change is a strength, even if it means plunging part of the company into total confusion for a while.

—Jack Welch

In the midst of movement and chaos, keep stillness inside of you.

—Deepak Chopra

Fear of another Great Depression has clouded our thinking ever since the recession that followed the attacks of September 2001. It is a fear we have all felt deeply—including me. After decades of working on the inside of corporate America, I started to have a hollow feeling about these companies of all sizes. I wondered what I had been working for all of these years, as I searched for real meaning in my work.

The world is a different place than it was only a few years ago. While our technology doubles in efficiency and complexity every single year, every single day people are inundated by the primal fear of terrorism, the potential failure of capitalism, and even our own government. Millions of concerned citizens receive regular e-mail about conspiracy theories concerning our national leaders and business figures—instead of good information with a hopeful premise. People watch the stock tickers daily, living and dying by the smallest movements in those little digital numbers at the bottom right of the television screen, instead of believing in the long-term longevity and prosperity of our markets. Many of us sit in wait for the day that our grandparents always warned us about. Everyone is anxious about the economy.

And yet, in many ways, the recession of 2008 to 2009 represented the greatest time of clarity that the world has seen in many decades. For centuries, we have been looking for the cutting edge in investment, hiring, business planning, and even sales floor leadership—in all the wrong places. We are now realizing with increasing clarity that the many ways we have been doing business over these past few generations has been fundamentally flawed. The clarity I am talking about is coming in the form of a major shift in how the world does business, and is pushing us into a new age in business, one of discovering the spiritual power that exists all around us in the workplace—whether we realize it or not. And it all starts when we open our eyes to see it.

I began to open my eyes after September 11, 2001, in the middle of the dot-com bust. You could just see the onset of greed snaking its way into the real estate and financial markets—under everyone's noses, but it was there. I also saw how, as a successful corporate executive, I myself was fitting snugly into the paradigm that allowed such practices to take place. These old ways did not seem to work all that well: major recessions that no one could predict were still coming; my corporate peers were receiving accusations of corruption and their ways of doing business were not even all that profitable; and every day, news about the business world was creating ripples of protests and demonstrations. I knew there had to be another way—and was I ever right.

Throughout this book, I go into significant detail about just what this shift is, what it means to see God in the workplace, and the exciting prospects that a new world of spirituality in business holds for you. But there are many simple things that you can probably see right now that should whet the soul of even the most skeptical person. The most successful companies in the world today are employing business tactics that just 20 years ago would have turned off even the most open-minded investors.

Without a single influential leader—without a Henry Ford or an Eli Whitney pushing his or her own personal new idea—a major wave of change has risen naturally from the tides of everyday business. Microsoft, Toyota, hedge funds, even the governments of China and India—the most successful economic drivers in the world today—now disregard the things about business that were once thought to be the key to success: protection of intellectual property, an "us versus them" mentality, bureaucratic R&D, and so forth. Instead, they are taking actions that would have been considered *crazy* a decade ago. A more thorough example of this can be found below in Tapscott and Williams's treatment of Goldcorp; but other open-source efforts between companies include the Human Genome Project and the release of the beta versions of software to thousands of users in advance of a program's official release by Google, Microsoft, and others.

One strong example is ExxonMobil, a company that once guarded its potential oil reserves like a state secret, yet who now partners with companies all over the world in order to access remote oil reserves (and other resources once thought impossible to access) more effectively. ExxonMobil is partnering with firms like Qatar Petroleum, the Angolan National Oil Company, Japan's Sakhalin Oil, and India's state-owned oil company ONGC Videsh Ltd. These associations force ExxonMobil to trust its proprietary technology and resource exploration techniques to others, in exchange for only what these local corporations can do for them. And all of this is happening naturally, as those among us who understand the rise of the new age are proving themselves to be the most efficient and powerful businesspeople out there.

It is a corporation's job to convince its shareholders that it uses all possible means to increase the value of their stock; however, most companies today only work at half throttle. Contemporary business culture has entirely overlooked the important spiritual assets it has within its grasp, causing the entire economy to suffer, especially considering that this critical asset lies *just beneath the surface* of the people who work within the halls of its building. But these spiritual assets have not been tapped, because they cannot be accessed with a snap of the fingers. These assets take time and patience to develop. It's not a matter of tweaking the balance sheet. Rather, these qualities lie at the heart of that feeling that people have long held as their most private and cherished personal attribute; the one thing with us from birth until death; and that which binds even the most disparate of personalities: our spirituality.

One example of an industry that has found great success utilizing more open and spiritual practices is the natural resource industry, in particular the mining, exploration, and resource extraction companies. Don Tapscott and Anthony Williams describe the story of mining company Goldcorp in their book *Wikinomics: How Mass Collaboration Changes Everything*. Up until 1999, natural resource companies' traditional ways of doing business was to keep all maps, statistics, and exploration results of their respective properties secretly to themselves.

However, Goldcorp ran into a problem that could not be solved by anyone within the company. It was running out of places to mine gold; and even though test drilling suggested that there was as much as 30 times more gold in its territories than it had been mining, the company was having trouble finding it. It could take decades to locate all the gold, so Goldcorp knew there had to be a better way of finding new ore. CEO Rob McEwan asked the head geologist to publicly release all of Goldcorp's geological data on its "Red Lake" property—as far back as 1948—and put it online. Despite pressure from inside the company to stop before things went too far, McEwan issued the "Goldcorp Challenge," offering prize money to anybody out there in cyberspace who could provide the company a better way of locating and accessing its gold reserves.[1]

The submissions, which came from everybody from physicists to computer analysts, flooded in. According to Tapscott and Williams, "The contestants had identified 110 targets on the Red

Lake property, 50 percent of which had not been previously identified by the company. Over 80 percent of the new targets yielded
substantial quantities of gold ... it helped catapult [McEwan's] underperforming $100 million company into a $9 billion juggernaut."[2]
Although the authors focus on this story for its use of open-source
information, I am interested in the candid approach that McEwan
used to transform his company into an international star. He used
several qualities—trust, honesty, and flexibility—in relationships
that had previously been secretive and uncommunicative. By doing
so, McEwan paved the way for other ideas. That the company owned
the property was enough to guarantee profits; by sharing information in this way, McEwan discovered previously untapped potential
in his company's relationship with the world.

Similar evidence of the rising awareness of spiritual assets in the
business world can be found in the culinary industry. After Nóbu
Matsuhisa opened his first restaurant in Beverly Hills, the restaurant
quickly went from obscurity to the toast of the town. Yet Matsuhisa
had no plans to expand "Nobu." The restaurant attracted a who's who
of Hollywood talent, including one loyal customer named Robert
De Niro, who two years after Nobu first opened, asked Matsuhisa
if he would partner with him to open a Nobu in New York City.
The actor even flew Matsuhisa out to Manhattan for a week, but
Matsuhisa was suspicious of taking on a partner. He had worked for
others for his entire life, dreaming of the day he would put his own
name on a sushi restaurant without being beholden to anybody. And
by all accounts, Nobu was doing quite well already—Matsuhisa did
not *need* help.

De Niro asked again four years later, having frequented Nobu
faithfully the entire time without any bad feelings toward Matsuhisa. Although De Niro never mentioned the rejection, he still
believed after four years that Nobu should start to expand to other
cities—starting with New York. The story goes that because De Niro
had waited patiently that entire time, Matsuhisa felt differently when
he heard De Niro's second offer. When asked what had changed his
mind—whether it was six long years of staying in one place, or
something else—Matsuhisa said instead, "I trust him because he was
waiting four years."[3]

It was De Niro's openness to Matsuhisa's needs and his respect for Nobu's autonomy that allowed this partnership to unfold. After the restaurant opened in New York, Nobu went on to become a chain of 25 well-reviewed, high-profile, world-renowned restaurants—without sacrificing an inch of quality. Nobu is now one of haute cuisine's best-known names. Nobu's road to success started with a different kind of deal making, one that was patient, had no built-in pressure, and required each party to be fully open to the other so that trust could grow between them. Goldcorp and Nobu are just two of many stories that demonstrate the power of spiritual practices when it comes to contemporary business.

In what sense are these examples of spirituality or God at work? The more skeptical reader will scoff; and it is true that my definition of spirituality is broader than most people's definition. Let me start to define it by asking you some questions. When a loved one dies, or you encounter one of those tragedies that we all endure at least once in our lives, where do you turn? Most likely you turn to your spirituality. Consider the lives of the greatest men who ever lived, from Aristotle to Einstein to Thomas Jefferson, and ask yourselves what they *themselves* attributed to their success. The answer inevitably comes back in the same form: their spirituality.

One finds that during the happiest moments of our lives, the word "spiritual" is perhaps the only one word that truly captures those moments when we relate them to others. It is at the core of what elevates us as human beings. To say, then, that spirituality has no role in business, our economy, our companies, our jobs—the key elements of the human experience—despite the central role it plays in all other aspects of our lives, is ridiculous. The question is not whether spirituality plays a role in our business and professional life, but rather *what* role it plays.

The most basic evidence for the spiritual realities in the workplace comes from the idea of consumer confidence, a fairly simple concept of economics. This concept refers to the confidence that a consumer has in the security of his or her job, the stability of his or her cash flow, and the accessibility of the products he or she wishes to buy. Consumer confidence levels have long been known to correlate with the economy's boom and bust cycle. When confidence is high, people spend money, and the economy soars. But when confidence is low, people become frightened; they spend less, save more, and the economy tumbles. Businesses make less money, which means that jobs are less stable, which leads to a vicious circle of uncertainty that drives consumer confidence lower and lower—a partial cause of any recession.

Consumer confidence is a spiritual matter because it is based on trust. When consumer confidence dips, it means that we are losing confidence in the economy; and if our collective purchasing habits are what comprise the economy, then we have really lost confidence in each other. We have stopped trusting that others will buy, so we feel like we should stop buying things, too; and while trust by itself is not the same as spirituality, it is an essential component. When we have more faith in one another, the economy improves; but when we have less faith in one another, the economy tanks.

Locally, cities that spend more time nurturing a Spiritual Environment—artistic, community-oriented, and open-minded— are the most innovative in the world. Dr. Richard Florida developed something called the Creativity Index, and though creativity is only a sliver of what I am talking about, this tool does provide one marker for the level of spirituality in a certain region. Florida's index takes into account what percentage creative workers like artists, researchers, and the like are of the total workforce; the number of patents filed annually per capita; the prevalence of high-tech industries. It is an index that is determined by the "area's openness to different kinds of people and ideas."[4] Openness, industrial advancement, creativity, and a focus on new ideas are all components of a Spiritual Environment.

After Florida determined the Creative Index for the United States' 49 regions—with more than 1 million people in total population (as of 2000)—he compared these rankings against only the high-tech and innovation rankings as they stood, independent of the index. He found that of the top 10 cities in his Creative Index, every city—except for Hartford (which ranked 13 out of 49 in terms of innovation) and Houston (which ranked 16 out of 49 in both categories)—ranked in the top 10 for either innovation or the prevalence of high-tech industries. These statistics point to a direct correlation between spiritual practices and innovation. On the other end of the spectrum, regions with a culture of closed, protected research and a service- (rather than creative-) oriented economy—like Las Vegas, Memphis, and New Orleans—all ranked near the bottom of the overall index, innovation ranking, and the high-tech ranking.[5]

On a corporate level, Paul Seabright wrote in his book *The Company of Strangers: A Natural History of Economic Life* that "What made Du Pont, General Motors, Standard Oil, Sears Roebuck, and US Steel different from other less successful firms was not that they had different technological opportunities, but rather that they had the organizational and managerial capacity to exploit those opportunities to the fullest. They supplemented the invisible hand of the market with the visible hand of management."[6] Organizations function best when all their parts have been "greased"—happy workers, satisfied managers, and an ecstatic clientele. Though many people do not realize it, this is a spiritually evolved organization.

The untapped spiritual assets I discuss define the next era of global business; yet they can only be attained by the individual. You are the only person who can realize them—nobody can do it for you. That puts the power to make the world a better, more profitable, and more stable place in your hands. The kind of power normally reserved only for those at the "top" is now shifting evenly to everyone throughout the system.

The Very First Transaction

To utilize these assets, you must start by understanding how spirituality fits into contemporary business methodology and nomenclature. This is a brief journey to the very brink of our human ancestry, where the concept of God first developed. Isaac Asimov once wrote that the discovery of religious thinking was preceded only by the discoveries of stone tools, fire, and walking on two feet, as humankind first began to reshape its own world. Anthropologists describe this era as one of tribes of men and women, huddling around human graves decorated by delicate food and flowers after the death of their kin. There was a sense among the mourners that life was bigger than death. These ancient ancestors of ours felt something powerful, and, I argue, more meaningful than even the democracy and modern economic theory that now organizes our world. This was humanity's first Spiritual Transaction: one with what lies beyond us. Their first transaction was with the dead.

In my view, the basis of all spirituality is the Spiritual Transaction:[7] an interchange between each of us and all those things beyond ourselves. Every prayer is a transaction between you and that which you feel has some sway over your life. Every Saturday or Sunday spent at service is a spiritual transaction in which you exchange your time in return for spiritual satisfaction, growth, and community. Tools and fire were things people used to satisfy our physical survival; but spiritual thinking was the first thing they used to satisfy the parts of them they felt but could not see.

The Spiritual Transaction is a framework that shows you the true nature of the relationship between spirituality and business. It reflects the physical laws of the universe; but it also leads to higher profits and a competitive advantage. The Spiritual Transaction represents the harsh realities of the economy as well as all the glorious success that is available to each of us.

The first Spiritual Transaction that I experienced was at Rosemount Engineering—now a division of Emerson Electric—at the beginning of my entry into the computer industry when I was 19 years old. I had been hired to operate a new computer that I knew nothing about. But as I stumbled through it, trying to figure things out, I was befriended by an aeronautical engineer who sensed some talent in me. He not only taught me how to do the job, he gave me the freedom and encouragement to learn how to program the computer myself. These were the days when a computer was worth millions of dollars and was the size of a room, so any failure on my part would have been a "little" more expensive than if I had been working with a computer in today's world.

This Spiritual Transaction—a human spirit–to–human spirit connection—launched my career in the nascent information technology industry, a career that later included leadership positions with Honeywell, GE, and other major companies. It taught me a new and selfless way of thinking in a novel industry, and for that I have always been grateful. Spiritual Transactions can be as simple as looking someone in the eye when he or she is talking and really paying attention to his or her needs; giving a helping hand before it is asked; or making sure something you appreciated does not go unnoticed.

Transactions are the basis of all business. You interact with others, exchange services and money, and build profit margins wherever you can. However, it is harder to see the spiritual origin of these transactions. The old adage that business is business and not personal, represents the culture people have developed to cut out the emotional aspects of business—in the mistaken belief that a good business should work like a functional machine.

In fact, spirituality is not something that needs to be put into business; it is the origin of business itself. Whether you consider the sacrifices of material goods to the gods of old, or simply laying a bouquet of flowers on the grave of a family member or friend, you are giving things to something invisible in exchange for an emotional feeling—a feeling of peace, closure, or hope. In business, you give material goods or services in exchange for other goods and services; however, the essence of those transactions is still in the feelings that they bring.

Nobu Matsuhisa struck his deal with De Niro because he felt comfortable. The Japanese economy is built on this kind of trust in many cases—deals between distributors last for decades, whereas many other companies are easily convinced to switch service providers if they are offered better terms. One of the reasons this can be faulty is that working with the current provider to improve delivery and cost measures is often more efficient and creates sturdier corporate infrastructure. If clients are constantly switching service providers, this incentivizes those providers to increase invisible costs in order to guarantee that each client becomes the best source of income possible in the short term. It also increases a provider's costs, which are passed on to its clients.

People move on stocks largely because of the swell of movement in the marketplace—mania—instead of the actual balance sheets behind the shares they are buying. Advertising and brand promotion hinges on forming an emotional bond between the product and the client. Employees work harder when they are feeling good, and slack off when they are feeling stressed out, anxious, or unhappy. A good deal makes you more comfortable, but even good risks are often not taken because of that "feeling" in the pit of your stomach. While the result of a transaction is often material, the transaction itself is purely *im*material; it is an agreement between two people. In order to improve the material results of your transaction, you must improve the transaction itself.

Understanding the Spiritual Transactions can be as easy as noticing that you feel badly when you are a part of a bad deal, and that you feel great when you strike a good deal. When a co-worker stabs you in the back during a project, you become upset; but when you work well with others and things get done, you are pleased and satisfied. Even skeptics know that emotional reactions affect your motivation and capacity to work. But the reality is that every material transaction has a deeper meaning than the monetary one. The problem is simply that people today have become numbed to this aspect of transactions after years of focusing solely on material gain in business.

The view that business and the economy can best be understood as impersonal machines is quickly being disproved by our modern economic order. Some people call it the "2.0 economy," claiming that it is information technology that is creating the new ground on which business should be run. I argue that these advancements are not the new infrastructure of business, but instead is a vehicle that is taking us back to an even more primitive and efficient way of doing business: unearthing the amazing potential of the spiritual core of our transactions. To see spiritual forces in action, just look around your workplace.

What defines those who really get ahead in life? A quick answer might be that these people are good networkers, as Malcolm Gladwell stated in his book *The Tipping Point*. But what *is* networking, other than forming relationships? And all good relationships fundamentally have a spiritually sound foundation. Another answer might be: these people are cool under pressure. But where does this calmness come from, other than a balanced personality, which at its core must also be spiritually sound.

Spirituality exists in business in a prereligious form, one of basic reciprocation and appreciation that has been lost only because it has been forgotten. When you look at an employee who saved the day, or just received that new promotion, you can often be tempted to say, "He makes it look so easy!" That is because tapping into the part of us that allows us to make spiritual transactions is the opposite of complicated; it is, indeed, easy. You just have to know how.

Here are two examples of the difference between handling business situations in a spiritual way and a nonspiritual way. First up: hiring new employees. A nonspiritual hiring might look like this...

The interviewer overplays the strength of the organization, and underplays the problems that the interviewee is expected to resolve. Compensation is pushed to the minimum. The employer shows little in the personal and family life of the candidate. Abilities and prior job successes are of primary interest, and the soft skills of interpersonal communications, work ethics, and teamwork are least important. There may be few other interviewers, none of whom particularly invite questions by the candidate. The interviewee is only interested in getting a job and getting it at maximum pay. He or she is essentially an expendable commodity in the eyes of the interviewer, and the job seeker is looking at a job, not a career. Both parties operate out of expedient self-interest. The likelihood of turnover and business difficulties is high, and the prospect of a long-term, successful relationship is low.

However, if the interviewer and the candidate concentrate on creating a Spiritual Transaction, the outcome might look like this...

Both the interviewer (particularly the hiring manager) and candidate pay much attention to the bonding agents of mutual respect, openness, and trust. They discuss their respective backgrounds and lives, in addition to the organization, its culture, and an honest appraisal of how the business is doing. Management and peers are the interviewers. An appropriate compensation package is provided, along with strong indoctrination, orientation, and training upon hiring. Managers and peers show genuine interest in the personal life of the candidate. The organization goes to great lengths to create a welcoming atmosphere and provide emotional support to the new hire. There is definite interest in a successful long-term relationship. It is likely that the business is already doing well, and that the interviewee will add to that success.

A second example of the simple application of the Spiritual Transaction model to everyday business comes from the sales call. A non-Spiritual sales call might look like this...

The salesperson is more interested in getting an order at all costs than he is in providing a great service to the prospect, let alone trying to bond with them. He applies strong pressure to get the appointment, and makes several assumptions about the prospect's needs. The salesperson openly belittles the competition, deflects the prospect's questions, and provides only incomplete and inaccurate information. The salesperson has done little or no research about the prospect's business or organization. He or she is not willing, or in many cases not capable, of building a long-term relationship with the prospect and his or her organization. The process is hit-and-run, and the chance of an order is low. Both the salesperson and the prospect leave the meeting disappointed. Politics in both the selling and the buying in the organizations are extreme.

However, a Spiritual sales call might look like this...

From the outset, the salesperson desires to find out what the prospect needs and what issues he wants to resolve. The salesperson takes great time and care to learn as much as he can about the prospect's business and organization. The entire process is low pressure and always open, honest, and trust-building. Both the salesperson and the prospect want a strong, long-term relationship that is profitable to both parties. All information provided is the truth, and any weaknesses are openly discussed. Both the salesperson and the buyer use a trusted team to assist the process, which then becomes a two-team effort to secure the best short- and long-term solution possible. A mutually profitable and enduring connection is made.

You might be thinking, "This doesn't sound very spiritual; it just sounds like good business." It is actually both! The basic principles here are simple, but the difference between a Spiritual Transaction and a non-Spiritual Transaction is huge.

There are many high-profile examples of where a switch to a Spiritual Transaction could have saved both parties of the transaction a lot of inefficiency, pain, and money. An extreme example is Merck's handling of prescription painkiller VIOXX. A series of hidden product weaknesses and disconnected consumer-producer relationships resulted in an alleged 27,785 deaths and 100,000 lawsuits, according to the FDA.[8] Merck spent almost $5 billion settling lawsuits. And this is simply a magnified case of what goes on in the corporate world every day. Though the scale is smaller in most cases, you can witness the effect of non-Spiritual Transactions on your customer base as well as your own experiences as a consumer.

Let us return to Isaac Asimov's take on the origin of the Spiritual Transaction. While he used the word "religious" in his scientific history,[9] instead of spirituality, to denote the rise of what I have identified as our first transactions, I believe that what he described in our ancient ancestors was not truly religion. Religion is a system that was developed to organize society before the arrival of democracy and free market commerce. These religions—first on the steppes of Asia and then ancient Mesopotamia—were spawned by the belief that there was something else outside of us that people could not fully understand. It was a philosophic pondering that occurred long before even the Greeks. It was not yet religion: this was pure spirituality.

Spirituality and religious thinking are similar. They both represent the transactions people make with their idea of God and, for many, with the dead. They also indicate what a person has decided about how he or she sees the immaterial or invisible nature of the world. For a spiritual person, this invisible nature might be a kind of universal intelligence. For the scientific person, it might be the unknown and unfelt laws of the universe at work.

In this book, I assume the mutual exclusivity of neither. Spiritual Transactions represent what makes sense to you in the face of a confusing world; your connections with that which you feel but cannot see. Spirituality is something with which you come to terms within yourself, while religion is something you come to outside of yourself. Spirituality is what you might call the temple inside of you; whereas religion is the temple you visit on holidays and weekends.

Just as you cannot know a "God" or yet understand all the laws of the universe, you cannot truly know what is going on inside the minds of those around you. Even with perfect communication, there are things to which you have no access. You cannot read your colleagues' minds; however, there is a basis to most of which you think and feel, and that is your belief system. You operate under a certain set of values, and regardless of what they are, they serve as your underlying spirituality. Most things that you do can be reduced to—or illuminated by—your spiritual foundation. At the core of this spirituality are simply concepts—you want to feel accomplished, you like it when others like you, you are looking for positive feedback from the world, and so forth. These are the elements of your personality that motivate your interactions with others. Therefore, your spiritual core is the place that each transaction originates.

Most transactions today, however, involve two spiritual cores that are not paying attention to one another, and therefore clash. Spiritual Transactions remove this clashing from the equation and allow transactions to occur fluidly. Spiritual Transactions are not some newfangled way of doing business, but rather interactions in their purest and most efficient form.

There are specific places where Spiritual Transactions are clearly more effective ways of doing business: deal brokering, employee interaction, management of people, sales, marketing, and many more. Deal brokering, for instance, is easier for everyone involved if people can find a way to communicate the *real* needs that the deal represents, and not just what is written down on paper. Employee interaction is more straightforward when people do not have to concern themselves with superficial and petty issues that obscure the essence of what everyone there is trying to accomplish. Management is made easier when employees feel that their needs are being met as much as the company's, which makes employees work harder and earn the company more money. Sales are completed more easily when salespeople connect their products with the natural desires of their customers. Each of these ideas revolves around accessing and utilizing the spiritual assets of the individual and the company at large, as is shown throughout this book.

Religious Science founder Ernest Holmes once wrote of this kind of interaction in his 1923 book, *Science of Mind*. He described the process of finding the most profitable kind of human transactions in saying that "the only inquiries we need to make are: Do the things that we want lend themselves to a constructive program? Do they express a more abundant life, rob no one, create no delusion, but instead, do they express a greater degree of livingness? ... If it is money, automobiles, houses, lands, stocks, bonds, dresses, shirts or shoestrings, cabbages or kings ... there can be nothing ... to deny us the right to the greatest possible expression of life. So we need not hesitate to use [this] for personal motives, for we have a perfect right to do so" (Holmes, 151).

Our Fear of a Religion of Commerce

In the early twentieth century, people were afraid that commerce was about to supplant Christianity and become a new religion for a new century. At the time, many began to worry that "Business is our God."[10] People really believed that because money was so important to them—and because businessmen were beginning to overtake the clergy in terms of social status—that business was about to make religion obsolete. Many people referred to the push toward the worship of money as a "cult of prosperity."[11] Modern capitalism's extreme success—as it began its journey to becoming a superpower—was seen as a great threat to all religion, for religion had long been the infrastructure of society—the role that business serves today. Much of what we believe about business and religion's relationship was born during the 1920s and 1930s: the idea that money and God are competing forces for our worshipful attention.

However, the connection between religious thinking and commerce is as old as the modern world itself. Most religions have a long history of encouraging their followers to give money (sometimes even money they did not have) to the church in an expectation of social acceptance, religious feeling, and even special treatment. Today, many people use credit cards and other forms of debt to still reach beyond their means in order to create that same sense of belonging and prestige. But instead of funding church projects and expansions, people buy material goods like cars, houses, electronics, and fashionable clothing. They contribute to the power of Coca-Cola and Walmart in their quest to cover the world with their logos and fill a place in people's hearts, rather than contributing to the ambitions of proselytizers who cross new lands in an effort to convert new peoples. They find satisfaction and a feeling of accomplishment in how people look at them in their new cars, rather than in the lauded admiration of the local priest for their hefty tithes. The world's obsession with image is far older than the corporate environment in which we now find ourselves.

Some might argue that modern culture is a materialization of the antique fear that commerce would supplant religion. It has even been stated that people today do indeed worship at work instead of at church. After all, even back then, church was usually more about shifting around in your seat and whispering to friends as the minister spoke on and on, instead of listening to what he actually had to say. At least at work we get swivel chairs.

But the truth is that this age of materialism has actually led to the resurgence of spirituality, and a new set of businesspeople who are naturally gravitating toward a different form of business—whether they know it or not. Alongside the new Gap store is a Yoga studio. Beside the latest trashy novel on our shelves, there is inevitably a book that has inspired us. Oprah follows midafternoon soap operas, and celebrities have henna tattoos on their hands instead of a cigarette between their fingers. With visions of future technology and lifestyles inevitably come visions of the Apocalypse and talk of a "Second Coming." It is sometimes difficult to see this, though, as people have historically associated a rise in spirituality with a resurgence of the church; and United States and European congregations have seen a steep decline in regular attendance over the past 50 years. New generations have cast off the tendrils of weekly services in favor of exploring purer religious thinking and spirituality on their own terms.

What most of us come to understand about the immateriality of the world is something closer to mysticism than a religious understanding. This takes us back to a time before the Temple of Zeus in Athens or the Temples of Karnak in Egypt; back beyond the hypnotic trance dances of India and Siddhartha, to a primal sense that there is something within us that not only lacks understanding, but is also underused. Whereas in prior centuries people have been taught quite strictly about what to make of these feelings and curiosities, changing social norms have allowed individuals the freedom to explore the more personal meanings of what goes on inside of each of us.

Business-as-religion never took hold of the United States and the other major world states in the way conspiracy theorists once feared it would; but those brief years are just one example of how spirituality and business have attempted, and failed at, amalgamation. Spirituality and business have a natural attraction. Like opposite sides of a magnet, they are eternally drawn to one another through their similar roots. They are flipsides of the most basic of all human concepts: the transaction. Yet the velocity with which one hurdles itself toward the other often makes a true understanding of their complementary nature nearly impossible. The speed of our epiphanies and the speed of commerce have, until now, disallowed a long exploration of their relationship.

Your world right now is incomplete if you do not take at least some time to understand the relationship between spirituality and business. It is impossible to work at full capacity, with efficiency and contentment, toward your lifelong goals and any overall plan if you do not understand this relationship. Your spirituality is possibly the most important part of your arsenal when trying to get ahead in life. It is a part of your toolbox whose shine has been buried away and exposed to the tarnish of misuse.

It is like trying to write with only your writing hand, and the other tied behind your back. In fact, try this now—to get a better sense of what is being discussed here. Try writing a few sentences with your dominant hand and put the other behind your back—instead of right next to the writing hand. Your writing slows down; you find it difficult to stabilize, and suddenly you realize how much you need your other hand. It provides unseen support that makes writing such an easy and smooth process. Your spirituality is like that other hand, that invisible support that makes things easier. Although you *can* physically write a paragraph with only one hand, it is far more difficult. Similarly, you can get through life without the invisible centering and support of an understanding of your spiritual assets; why would you want to put yourself through such an unnecessary trial?

We are not taught in business school to use the spiritual part of ourselves, and there are no orientation courses for new employees that stress this asset's importance. You cannot rely on your employer or any existing system of educating new businesspeople to provide you with such an education. Meanwhile, your reverend or your priest—should you have one—is trained in spiritual ideas, but not in the rigors of the business world. In order to learn more about your most important assets, you need help from a source that you do not often go to—yourself. Accessing your spiritual side is much like trying to find someone to marry; there is nothing in the traditional path of your education that will teach you anything about dating. There is not a school you can go to, nor a structural path to follow, that will bring you to that perfect state of bliss where you finally realize that you are in love—possibly for good. There are no courses that teach you about the role spirituality can play in getting you to that next level in business either. In fact, most of the important things you can learn in life can never be read in a textbook.

One business model created in the 1980s called the Ghoshal/Bartlett model came close to something that could be used. Professor Sumantra Ghoshal of the London Business School saw a particular need to pay attention to nature and the natural laws of the universe when developing new theories of management. Around this time, many gurus and professors in India were noticing strong similarities between their age-old philosophy and Hinduism, and new branches of popular physics like quantum mechanics. Ghoshal talked about the role people played in the "control mix" rather than "hierarchy."[12] His theories, and those of his contemporaries, made them among the hottest business gurus by the 2000s, though Ghoshal would sadly die before witnessing the true rise of his ideas. His belief that business should be a force for good in the world was a controversial one right up until his death. Ghoshal was one of the first academics to really feel the shift toward a new age in business: an era of business *grounded within our spirituality.*

Some books focus on all facets of spirituality, but they gloss over the professional part of your life. Yet in this day and age of uncertainty—when your job is not as secure as you thought it was or your job is not quite what you hoped it would be—your spirituality might just be the most important piece of you. Not because it can get you through the rough days, but because it can create the better days for you and ensure that the worst of times stay far away from your doorstep. The great news is that you are born with spirituality and you can *always* learn more about it. In fact, every experience you have in life—including the business-related ones—is a spiritual experience that reveals the true nature of yourself unto you.

Whether present at birth or realized soon afterward, our spirituality is not just the oldest thing we have ever known as a civilization: it is also the thing we have known longer than anything as individuals. Our imaginary friends as children, our curiosity about the world, our belief in things much more impressive than what we see in our immediate surroundings—these are all part of our earliest Spiritual Environment. It is stunning when we consider that the most important aspects of being an employee in this era of the information age are things that we have had right from the start, whether we have nurtured them, even before we learned to read and write.

Spirituality's role in business is not something that makes itself readily apparent. I myself did not fully sense its presence until the late 1990s, even though it was already inside of me. As I became more aware of it, the phenomena of the Spiritual Transaction increasingly showed up in my work, though I did not yet know what it was called. How amazing to discover this untapped, infinite resource—and how fantastic the results in my businesses: a more satisfied and harmonious organization, greater profitability, and significant contributions to local and global humanity! Yet the importance of spirituality in business is not already a widely known phenomenon of grave importance, and the world economy has, for all intents and purposes, become a miracle of human innovation in spite of this.

Think, though, of the example of a librarian during the early 1990s who was given the long and arduous task of transferring all of the data from Dewey decimal card catalogs into the school's new computer. If, say, the computers of the time had proven themselves worthless and people all went back to the card system—what would have been the use of transferring the data into the computer system? Can you really be so sure about the value of spirituality in business?

Spirituality has already proven its mettle as the next big shift in business culture in many ways that I cover moving forward. The world's most exciting companies and individuals have stumbled upon it, or have made it a core aspect of planning their futures. It is important to realize that the time of wondering about the value of spirituality is over. Many grade schools still refused to transfer their library catalogs many years after computer systems proved to be a Godsend; we must ensure that the mature business world does not follow in a similar vein. The world cannot allow itself to be discouraged from yet another great advance simply because of a little inconvenience.

As a businessperson, I feel that everyone should get this kind of lazy doubt out of the way right here at the beginning of this conversation. I can tell you from experience that there is significant evidence that spirituality in business is more than important; it is vital, and has proven itself as such through the lives of many people like myself as well Over the course of the following chapters, you will see just how critical spirituality is.

One argument the skeptic might have of spirituality's role is in the plain fact that business is often very ugly. Serious deals and business plans are not always pretty. People get hurt. Business is essentially the competition for resources and finances, which means that somebody has to get left behind. The world is a selfish place, but what is this selfishness that our motivations and intentions rest upon?

If you cannot make yourself happy, then how do you expect to make others happy? If you do not have the funds to drive your own business, then how do you expect to contribute something to society? Capitalism works on the premise that your own selfish intentions will eventually lead to overall prosperity. Yet most of your contemporary transactions are missing a key element: their origin in spirituality. The spiritual assets that are used to make transactions more complete and efficient have been left out of the equation. Transactions can and do still exist without their spiritual components, but they create imbalance. Not everybody gets everything they want, which creates friction. Less efficient transactions use more energy, money, and time than they have to, which means that there is less of everything to go around. It is this principle that creates the excess within the business world at the expense of everybody else.

Poverty, for example, is a side effect of non-Spiritual Transactions. Companies and governments have to work harder—and therefore use up more resources—than necessary to get things done because their transactions are inefficient. These excess resources are drawn out of the pool of total resources—money, time, attention—that are held within the entire economy. Those not involved in business end up getting less out of the world, because they cannot compete for the resources available as effectively as businesses and businesspeople. Proof can be found in the capital-output ratio theory of contemporary economists: a nations' growth and success is directly related to how much money or other resources are required to produce one unit of product, as compared to previous and future years. The more resources that are required to create an economy's products, the less resources (energy, labor, capital, and so forth) there are to spread around.

Poverty comes from, among other things, inefficiency, as does unemployment. Employment numbers are directly related to the growth rate of an economy. Okun's Law states that for every 3 percent dip in GDP growth, you see a 1 percent rise in unemployment; and while there are other theories on the exact correlation between growth and unemployment, the rule reflects a definite truth about the economy. The more efficient your economy and businesses are, the more growth occurs. During a time of recession, the most important thing at stake is consumer confidence. Spiritual Transactions guarantee the most fluid, efficient flow of resources among people, companies, and even across international borders, as are seen throughout the book. It is no surprise then that those things that are associated with restricting your spiritual self—fear and doubt—are the things that rise with a recession and fall during boom times.

Resources are created by work. Oil comes from the ground because people drill for it and draw it up to the surface. Telephones exist because people monitor the machines that create them, construct telephone lines across the country, and then form companies to bring service to the lines. The more resources there are available to each of us, the more value there is in the world, and, therefore, the more value there is to go around. The only way to increase this value is to increase the efficiency of the work getting done. Non-Spiritual Transactions automatically reduce the efficiency of our work (through enhancing our anxieties, decreasing cooperation, giving us distractions, and discouraging innovation, among other things), which means that less value is created. This makes everybody poorer, no matter how we slice it. That efficiency is related to economic growth and quality of life is not a new concept; however, the discovery that Spiritual Transactions can radically improve the world is the notion that has always sat just beneath the surface of our intellects without ever really pushing through.

Once you see the merit of a widely available asset, you suddenly see the entire system as underperforming without it. And from a shareholder's point of view, no amount of underperformance is acceptable. Each and every one of us is a shareholder of the human race. We each have stock in the future of who the human race is. The human race is a society that has been underperforming for centuries. The global economy suffers because of it. Surprisingly so, because our spiritual assets are right there, just beneath the surface.

There are many examples of corporations trying to wring these spiritual assets—or something close to them—from their employees. Whether you are looking at the company-designed midafternoon nap chambers or meditation seminars, old-school corporate retreats or casual Fridays, it is all geared to making workers to feel more comfortable at work. It is aimed at encouraging those assets that lie within our spiritual selves to shine through. Employers, leaders, and managers are trying to elicit something that they believe can be inspired; yet spirituality is something deep within us that is not related to anything our boss can say, unless we are open to the word—and the words happen to be the right ones.

As for a little background on myself: I am a man of the corporate world. For decades, I served in top managerial and executive positions at some of the United States' best companies and many early start-ups. Across the board I have seen how business works. I can also say that by the year 2000, I was feeling increasingly drained of my normal high energy for work. I was feeling futile and had a sense that I was wasting my time in the traditional, and about to be battered, corporate world. I was equally tired of trying to fill the hole in my soul with material stuff as my "rewards" for success—homes, cars, and international travel—were no longer satisfying. Then, in 2001, I was offered a unique opportunity. I had belonged, for a while at that point, to a transdenominational, interfaith organization called Unity, which embraced spirituality from all over the world—from Buddhism to good old, home-bred, Conservative Christianity. And Unity was looking for a new CEO. This book was literally born out of my combined corporate and spiritual leadership experiences I had as a member of Unity, and as its president and CEO.

In 2001, I became president and CEO of Unity, for which I handled the publishing and other commercial wings of the Unity Movement, as well as noncommercial sectors like the Silent Unity prayer team and spiritual education. Through my six years of experience in this job, I saw how spirituality and business came together into a fluent and helpful organization that served millions of people, most of whom are professionals. When forced to look at spirituality and business as complementary aspects of the same idea, I started on a long journey of realization. It is from this experience and similar ones of those around me that I was able to learn a lot about the integral role of this most underused asset: spirituality at work.

Many people nowadays advocate treating themselves and acting like a corporation in order to get ahead. This is not a good way of seeing things. You are essentially intertwined with everyone around you on a far more personal level than any corporation is with its partners and competitors. In addition, corporations are run inefficiently and create immense value only by using countless resources to get there. Seeing yourself as a fellow shareholder—with me and everybody else—will greatly affect how proactive you are about what is going on around you, and how well you do for yourself. It is give and get: a transaction, if you will.

The Bottom Line

1. The Spiritual Transaction is a framework that allows the true nature of the relationship between spirituality and business to shine into a new economy at every level: individual, group, organization, corporate, national, and global.

2. The world's market systems and our economy were founded on the nature of the Spiritual Transaction.

3. Spirituality in business is not the same thing as religion in business.

2

CREATING MORE COMPETITIVE COMPANIES AND A HAPPIER YOU

I cannot remember a time when the Golden Rule was not my motto and precept, the torch that guided my footsteps.

— James Cash Penny

Do unto others as you would have them do unto you.

— Jesus Christ

Absolute Proof of Our New Era in Business

The spiritual root of business is not the only corrupted and forgotten aspect of how our markets work today. There is also a scientific root on which business practices have been based for nearly 400 years, but has now become obsolete. After I left Unity in 2007, Dr. Charlotte D. Shelton took over as president and CEO. She wrote a lot about the changing face of the world's markets. When she was assistant professor of management in the Helzberg School of Management at Rockhurst University, she wrote that many of the things that our world was based on for hundreds of years should have been changed long ago.

Dr. Shelton insists that the shift in business culture occurring now actually should have taken place at the beginning of the past century when Isaac Newton's view of the rules of how the world works were replaced by Albert Einstein's ideas, and ultimately, quantum physics. The world's scientists initially grumbled about the ideas in physics itself; however, they soon adapted their theories to the new rules that Einstein and his peers had laid out for them. Yet Dr. Shelton explains that organizational thinking has revolved around the work of a different physicist for centuries—the work of Isaac Newton. Dr. Shelton wrote that "Newton frequently characterized the universe as a great clock-like machine and his machine metaphor was transferred to the workplace. Organizational charts were designed to look like the schematics of a great machine and managers attempted to create results by managing employees as if they were mechanistic cogs."[1]

By the time that Newtonian physics were cast aside, people had forgotten that more than just scientific theories were based on Newton's laws. Corporate and business organizational practices founded on this faulty theory of linear thinking had been around for centuries, and consequently were *never changed*. Companies have always tried to be scientific about their businesses, thinking that natural laws were a good basis on which to rest their hopes. They were right. Their proposals were crafted around natural principles that were the best they had at the time. But after Einstein's revolutionary discoveries and the new physics that followed, there were suddenly much better principles to review. But to this day, companies have yet to truly explore the momentous opportunity for business communities to become more in tune with the natural state of the world—opportunities that provide even more evidence for the power and importance of the Spiritual Transaction.

Seeing business as a lever and pulley system—something self-contained and in which people's roles are always well defined—has created some of the great ills of our times. Patriarchal systems that promote only those with longevity within a company—while stifling bright ideas from newcomers—are borne of this theory of "how business should work." Systems that view longer hours instead of more effective work hours as the best way to increase output created the nightmarish conditions of Charles Dickens's industrial England. This system also emphasized the notion of slavery—gaining 24-hour access to a person's labor for minimal cost—as the only way to maximize company resources. Managers could never truly fix a problem within a company, because they could not access the motivations behind the people under them; they could only try to force a new result out of them. This system has led to a culture of bad bosses and the fear of the whims of the big kahuna at the top. It has led to distrust and to a belief that absolute power corrupts absolutely.

In 1995, I was affiliated with a now-defunct NASDAQ technology company called MTI, whose company culture was the exact opposite of that at Rosemount Engineering where I had first stumbled on the idea of a better transaction. The atmosphere at MTI was filled with fear instilled by a nonspiritual style of communications—incomplete, ungrounded, and untrusting. The right information could not make it to the right people at the right time, and clients were turned off by the way business was being done. The atmosphere there made it difficult to get anything done. One trying experience I remember vividly occurred when the senior field salespeople got together to convince the CEO that it would be a good idea to change the new product priorities based on their latest sales calls. The CEO allowed the long-term planning of the company to fall victim to constant tweaking, when every little bump along the way was fully absorbed into the system instead of acting as the vehicle's shocks, cushioning the company's direction. The company began to spin out of control, and after a couple of fast rises and sudden falls, it ultimately collapsed and was delisted from NASDAQ in 2007.

There was simply no logical process to follow at MTI. In order to get new products out, marketing and engineering employees had to do a great deal of work. However, the salespeople were requesting that we begin entirely new projects before we were able to complete the last one, which left all of the new products half-done and hindered our ability to get something out to market. This disconnect between the salespeople's inability to appreciate their requests' ramifications—and the fact that the CEO enacted them anyway—never made it into the balance of management's decision making. Although the salespeople's actions might have made sense if all the products were available to them more quickly, in reality, it hurt the company and made our jobs far more difficult. I found it impossible for me to work with the marketing and engineering people to stabilize a launch schedule for any new products. Products were so late that the actual launches ground to a halt. With just a little more communication and a shifting of priorities, those products could have made it to market on time. But instead, we were just banging our heads against the same wall over and over again.

How can a company believe that it is maximizing its potential if you, as an employee, do not feel safe? Your anxiety will not make you work more efficiently; at most, the anxiety will increase your speed at the expense of your quality. You might even try to manipulate the other people in your workplace in order to gain favor over others, instead of working with colleagues in a fluid manner. This stems from the fact that any non-Spiritual Transactions within a company use up many resources that are better used in cooperative projects. Less efficient companies have more blame to spread around and less credit to share. And this limited praise results in cutthroat competition between employees and damages cohesiveness. When there is less financial credit to go around, you see a breakdown in the fluidity and growth of the economy.

Fewer avenues to express your ideas to management and to help the company reach its potential creates cutthroat competition for the scarce attentions of those in charge. If you have a good idea, you then have to spend excess energy that could be put to better use. You not only have to come up with the idea, but then you also have to figure out a way of getting the idea into the right hands. You become guarded with your good ideas, because you are afraid that the ideas may get stolen or that someone else will get the credit for them. When credit is a scarce commodity, you create an environment where nothing new ever comes forward and a hundred great ideas are lost every single day. And as it did during my time at MTI, the scarcity of credit also creates fear.

Employees worry that if new ideas are "wrong" they will fall harder than they might in an open and enriched environment. This is not only management's fault. Just as the employee is competing for a smaller amount of praise, management is busy rationing its own smaller pool of resources, because workers are not working as hard or efficiently as they can. An employee wasting valuable efforts on a failed idea creates a dearth of resources that cannot be made up, so companies rely only on proven products, proven methods of doing business, and proven ways of making sales. These companies do not have the resources to innovate and are constantly vulnerable to the threats that smaller organizations pose, because these smaller organizations do have access to such resources. Spiritual Transactions increase innovation, which in turn makes management easier, which creates a better work environment, which, again, increases innovation.

So what would an organizational method based on newer science be like? Dr. Shelton writes that these methods are founded on newer physics, and states that a quantum-based organization promotes constant improvement and learning.[2]

Wait a second.... things are starting to get a little more complicated here. Let us try to break this down a little bit before I go further. What exactly is Dr. Shelton talking about?

Society learned, long after Newton had been gone, that the particles that make up our universe do not just move in a straight line and react in a perfectly predictable way. In fact, if you get way down to the itty-bitty most basic components of your body's molecules, you will find that the world acts quite improbably. Particles suddenly disappear and then reappear far from where they started. Little particles blink in and out of being without rhyme or reason, yet their totality leads to your stable and organized existence. The world's substance is constantly being re-created over and over again in entirely unique and creative ways. Like snowflakes, no two moments in time are ever the same, and yet time flows forward, forever uninterrupted.

In short: The rules of the world are not as cut and dry as Newton had said they were. Einstein's discoveries about what was really going on at the most basic level led us to believe that there must be something beyond the physical. Some religions, like Hinduism, took these discoveries as evidence that science was wrong, until science started to support their belief system and prove that they had always been right. There is no real evidence to back this up, although science today has a tougher time explaining the way things work in such definitive terms. Nothing is a theory; everything is a hypothesis.

But how does this statement relate to spirituality in business, the economy, and organizational practices? As Dr. Shelton explained, we have centered our organizational schematics on the idea that the natural order of things was based on a cut and dry, visible set of physical laws. Yet we now know that the universe actually operates under a far more exciting set of rules. Even the particles that make up our bodies' own molecules are constantly changing from one form into the next. So if we were to continue to base organizational ideas in the laws of nature, it would become apparent that *change and flexibility are far more important than certainty*. Society saw great advances when it built its market systems on the science of Newton. We have the opportunity today to see even more drastic, exponential changes in the prosperity of the world that follows these new natural laws of organization.

Spiritual Assets: Intuition, Imagination, Ingenuity

As I once recited in a lecture, former CEO of General Electric Jack Welch believes that "Predicting is less important than reacting."[3] If management has always been based on laws of nature—and these laws now point to the importance of adapting our business practices more easily, and these are assets provided to us by our spirituality—well, you get the picture. This is just one thing that supports the importance of our Spiritual Assets in the business world. The basis of all business itself now points to it.

Spiritual Assets are the parts of you that allow Spiritual Transactions to take place. Spiritual Assets are the elements that benefit and grow from Spiritual Transactions. A Spiritual Transaction is unlikely to strengthen, for instance, your greed or tendency to take revenge on those who have hurt you. But trust grows with Spiritual Transactions, as does your impulse to integrate your ideas into the projects you are completing. They are the parts of you from which the Spiritual Transaction originates.

A great example can be seen in the story of Michael Phelps, widely known today as the greatest Olympian who ever lived. However, what is less well known is that just before the 2004 Summer Games in Athens—where his first eight Olympic medals were won—Phelps made a life-changing decision. Bob Bowman, the coach for whom Michael had been swimming since he was 11 years old, was offered a job as head coach of the University of Michigan swim team. Bowman had realized when Phelps was young that he had the potential to be a great athlete. Before Phelps was even a teenager, Bowman had purposely targeted him for special training. Raised by a single mother and surrounded by sisters, Phelps looked to Bowman as a father figure. Bowman was more than just his coach. Phelps described him as, "My coach, yes. But he was also much, much more. A friend, yes, but still more than that. Bob had changed not only how I swam but who I was as a person, reminding me constantly how much love and dedication he has for the sport and everyone in it."[4] But with Bowman moving to Michigan, Phelps could not continue to swim under him if he stayed in his hometown of Baltimore. So as soon as Bowman told Phelps that he was taking the job, the first words out of Phelps' mouth were: "I'm going with you."[5]

There are two important lessons here. The first lesson is to understand that it is unlikely that Phelps would have ever attained the heights he did without the special care that Bowman provided. Phelps did not come from a place where Olympians were typically born; he suffered from ADHD in childhood and could have easily taken a different, more ordinary turn. Just months before Athens—where Phelps would first become a legend—Bowman had to leave. But because of Bowman's years of dedication to the swimmer—and the Spiritual Transactions he practiced day after day—their relationship was so strong that Michael followed him to Ann Arbor. Not only did Michael benefit, but instead of simply watching Phelps attain superstardom from a distance after almost a decade of working with him, Phelps ensured that Bowman would come along for the ride.

This dedication to their relationship built the trust and extraordinary physical stamina that they each shared through hard work and a hefty dose of Spiritual Transactions. The physical manifestation was astounding, yes; but so was the way their transactions manifested themselves in that fateful choice. Phelps named seven things that got him through those Athens games and on to accomplish the feat of winning eight gold medals in Beijing. Perseverance, belief, determination, confidence, courage, will, and commitment[6]—these were the qualities to which he attributed his success. While the weight training, certain practice sets, and even his genetics allowed him to swim fast, Phelps feels that these Spiritual Assets are what made him the fastest of all time. He wrote that Bowman's coaching philosophy was: "We do the things other people can't, or won't, do."[7] They are able and willing to do those things because of the strength of their Spiritual Assets, developed over the years through their Spiritual Transactions. And just as this has worked in sport, so, too, it works in business—as so many aspects of performance and leadership do.

I taught a class in July 2001 at Unity of Tustin called "Spirit, Science & Business" based on the work of Margaret Wheatley where I paraphrased her as saying: "Many organizations feel they have to defend themselves even against their employees... we are afraid of what would happen if we let these elements of the organization recombine, reconfigure, or speak truthfully to one another... fluctuation and change are essential to the process by which order is created."[8] Wheatley's assertion is a clear example of how old thinking can harm an organization. Fear of one another is a symptom of the old ways. When there is a certain "structure," we look for someone to step out of bounds. In addition, the certainty we desire from our prior organizational structures had always been impossible because at the end of the day, humankind bet the farm on Newton—*and Newton was wrong*.

Newtonian organizations typically did not welcome any new spark of inspiration that seemed to buck the system. When business is treated like a machine, fresh ideas are often considered to be flaws rather than improvements. If the system is designed to stay the same in perpetuity, then it is far too inflexible to change. Recessions occur without any real way of wriggling out, because the business practices that lead to them are stagnant. New organizations with better products create unimaginable competition for even the most successful firms, because the old dogs just cannot change quickly enough to keep up. Yet when the system is set up to *embrace* change, suddenly innovation does not have to fight its way into prominence the way it always has. Older companies can remain competitive and responsive to the historical economic patterns that affect their bottom lines.

Once the world had established its Newtonian systems of organization, it became far more concerned with keeping the smaller parts of the machine in line. Most of the innovations the world has developed have come about in this way. For instance, a significant invention like the computer emerges through the ideas of people *outside* the mainstream. Companies then spend decades working on just that one part of the machinery. Computer firms spend immense amounts of energy on the product itself, often utilizing a complete overkill of resources. Before computers, companies spent decades perfecting replaceable parts and mass production methods. Instead of keeping an eye out for complementary products, companies are content to simply fine-tune their current products until the products are forced into obsolescence by a new replacement that forces the system to change.

This kind of thinking has led the global marketplace to ruin. New, less structured economies—filled with freshly educated people who have been cultured by the latest realities of our world—will trounce on anyone who stands in their way. These organizations and the economies in which they operate are not based in the Newtonian systems of old; they are readily embracing the new "quantum" business paradigms. Much of the Western world has fallen far behind in terms of corporate innovation and changing business structures, which is another reason why the Spiritual Assets are so important—they allow you to keep up with the world. Without utilizing these assets, the organizations of which you are a part can no longer move into or stay in the lead, especially because the quantum business model is almost entirely composed of the use of Spiritual Assets through Spiritual Transactions.

My first experience with a quantum business was with a firm called Courier Systems. Its organizational structure was fairly flat, which allowed information to flow more easily and allowed for less stifling politics to develop. This configuration also allowed management to be extremely available to the staff and to permit communications to flow freely. The relationships between management and employees were built on trust. The independent work of everyone involved yielded incredible results. The firm was able to compete against the likes of IBM and attract the interest of corporate giant ITT, whose acquisition of Courier yielded the shareholders an extravagant return on their investment. I realize today that this organization had in fact thrived on Spiritual Transactions, and was indeed a *quantum business* before the term had even been devised.

There is a lot of fear out there that other nations like China or conglomerate powers like the European Union are about to overshadow the United States' ability to dominate the financial markets. Yet if the traditional economies of the West bring this new asset of spirituality into play, there is no telling how much longer they might remain the leader of the world. Spirituality has deep roots in capitalism's history, yet it is something with which most companies have lost touch over time. Although some modern industries have already developed around these quantum ideas—as are explored later in this chapter—something is still missing. The spirituality that had a place in the old economy and that should fit so well in our new economy is stilted, along with the majority of our businesses. Even the largest U.S. corporations are collapsing under the weight of this new competition.

This is not the first time in history that such a shift has occurred. Newton's ideas are only 400 years old. Before that time, humanity's greatest sense of the rules of the universe was informed by religion and religiously angled philosophy. Humankind did not believe it had long-term control over any aspect of its lives, because the whims of the gods could alter things in an instant.

Businesses during this time were built on a premise similar to the "known rules" of the universe. The greatest economic gains in the Middle Ages came from Imperial conquest. Merchants created vast trade networks that were often subsumed by war instead of retaken by adversarial powers. Humankind naturally designed networks to sustain its populations and improve daily life, but corruption and betrayal were rampant. Workers were brutalized and often enslaved by the elite and lost control over their lives until they united in the twelfth century. Even then, slavery and abusive sales practices were the norm.

The world changed dramatically when Newtonian business practices came into play. Humanity started to see economics and businesses as practices over which they had long-term control—control that gave way to order and rules, which eventually led to the abolition of slavery and the introduction of the consumer society. Without these changes, it is likely that civilization would never have achieved all that it has. Today we all stand on the precipice of yet another change that has the potential to radically alter humankind's destiny.

Just as the Industrial Revolution began about 100 years after Newton made his discoveries, our society has just surpassed the 100th anniversary of the Theory of Relativity. Now is the time for a total revolution in the way the business world works. Just as the Newtonian age of business transcended the limitations and tragedies of a religion-centered view of the universe and of business, so, too, is the world now transcending the laws of Newton and the business practices based on his ideas.

At the end of the day, we not only have a contemporary way to think about business, we need to think about spirituality in a new context as well. The roots of Newton's laws were used to organize our companies and in the way that we organized our religious infrastructure. Go to church on Sunday, call the minister over to dinner during the week, and see spirituality as an absolute truth taught in absolute books written by perfectly inspired people. Just as new industries are supplanting old corporations stuck in their Newtonian models, spirituality is starting to thrive, whereas churches are slowly losing influence.

Spirituality is a broad-ranging subject matter. I do not necessarily refer to any particular part when I call it an asset, but there are definitely some aspects to spirituality that are more important in terms of integrating of spirituality and business. Jean-Paul Sartre once wrote through the voice of one of his characters that "Every Sunday I used to go to Mass. Monsieur, I have never been a believer. But couldn't one say that the real mystery of the Mass is the communion of souls? A French chaplain, who had listened, standing, our heads bare, and as the sounds of the harmonium carried me away, I felt myself at one with all the men surrounding me. Ah, Monsieur, how I loved those Masses. Even now, in memory of them, I sometimes go to church on Sunday morning."[9] Sartre shows us that spirituality represents more than the ultimate transaction; it also symbolizes people's ultimate communion. Just as we seek profits together in our companies, we also seek a path forward for our respective countries, the global community, and a truer understanding of our world together. No wonder, then, that the laws of the physical world seem to find themselves the basis of our economic theories. The search for the role of spirituality is a challenge each of us faces.

Another tenet of early-twentieth-century business—aside from Newton's influence—was the idea that there was no such thing as cooperation between countries. Have you ever heard someone call himself or herself a "Realist"? This word actually refers to the dominant thinking of about a hundred years ago (based on ideas from the 1500s), which stated that there could be no cooperation between states (or people for that matter). Only competition and anarchy existed in the international system. Some people say that this idea has been quashed by modern globalization. I say that it was disproved long ago by the success and long life of the world's major transnational corporations. Even while nations were fighting among each other, companies worked together and spanned international borders despite the political conflicts that existed within their respective societies.

Yet our economy has long been convinced that hyper-competition is the only way to ensure growth. We used to think that the threat of failure—and the motivation of making it to the top—was necessary to ensure innovation. I believe that free market, capitalist systems have always been at the top not because of their specific systems, but because of the long-held spiritual root that gave birth to them. The higher level of education, size of population, and the initial incorporation of the currency that comes from these increases into our economy sets us apart, not some theory cooked up by politicians and academic ideologues.

Suspicion and blind competition may have been good enough in a Newtonian world, but modern people have discovered that flexibility and originality in business and lives is more reflective of the true nature of the world. In this new age of cooperation between nations and free trade, the asset of spirituality has never been so crucial. Its ability to bring even enemies together in the spirit of advancing the human race can come from no other place. If we are truly all shareholders of humankind, then we cannot afford to overlook spirituality in our overall plan. Individuals must seek a new paradigm of the broadest and deepest definition of success. We should seek a new kind of economy at all levels, including the individual, the group, the organizational, the corporate, the national, and the global.

The Cost of Human Capital versus Spiritual Capital

I have discussed the old way of doing things, where organizational methods treated employees less like people and more like cogs in a wheel. Yet beyond the idea that the foundation of these leadership practices is just plain wrong, what is the human cost of utilizing such principles today? An example of this can be found in the corporate giant Renault, one of the largest automobile companies in Europe.

Renault began a drastic turnaround when, in 2005, newly appointed CEO Carlos Ghosn was hired to launch the corporation in a brand new direction and make it the most competitive auto company in all of Europe. The asset on which Ghosn relied most for this push was the company's labor hours, which he steadily increased until the stress was almost too much for any employee to bear. But the worst place to work after Ghosn's arrival was the design center, for the company would live or die by the amount of innovation coming from within its walls.[10] Many of the employees approached management to tell them that the workers were becoming deeply depressed as a result of their radically altered life. Employees had no time for friends or family, or even to run the most basic errands to keep their home life in order because Ghosn demanded exasperatingly long hours filled with highly stressful work.

Ghosn was brought in to save a company that had been floundering in the newly globalized economy, yet his work is an example of how an old-school management style tends to just damage companies even more. Ghosn used the Newtonian model of management and corporate structure, which assumes that each cog in the wheel can simply be sped up in order to improve production, that every person can simply be pressured into better results if the right lubricants are in place. It is unlikely that concerns about employee stress were apparent to Ghosn, who himself was working around the clock. And even if they *were* a concern, a massive organization with more than 60,000 employees stuck in a Newtonian top-down structure tends to lose most complaints in the system.

In fact, corporate management might not have heard any objections about the working conditions if several employees had not been found, one by one, *dead*. One employee, to whom the authorities referred only as Raymond D., was found with a noose around his neck and the words "Tell Mr. Ghosn I can't handle the pressure anymore" written in a note on his body. Over the course of a year and a half, six employees at the design complex attempted suicide—and all but one succeeded. Two of the employees did so while on Renault property, leaving their co-workers with the horror of finding their lifeless bodies.[11]

Ghosn was quoted at the time as saying, "I am trying to motivate people to want to do more than they thought they could ... I was certain that everybody in the company would feel that they were doing something extraordinary by helping … achieve what we set out to accomplish."[12] Ghosn was smart enough to realize the value of a Spiritual Asset like motivation, yet these assets cannot be accessed through traditional, Newtonian methods. Instead, his attempt to speed up the system had deadly results.

Renault's situation also expresses the dangers of mixing traditional organizational methods and contemporary lifestyles. Ghosn's attempts to tap into his employees' Spiritual Assets caused those assets to disappear almost entirely from the workplace through the advent of extreme stress and emotional tension. By pouring more work on top of them in an attempt to find the corporate machine's stress saturation point, Ghosn gave the world an example of just how antiquated our old style of management has become. The importance of Spiritual Assets is something that eludes many leaders, merely because they have never been properly defined, but Spiritual Assets consist of more than the belief that people can work even harder than they did before.

A traditional response to Renault's story is simply that there needed to be less workload on the employees' shoulders, and that Ghosn should have hired more people instead of squeezing every last drop from the people he already had. But the extreme emptiness felt by some of Renault's best workers that led to their suicides reveals something more—that the work these men were doing could not fulfill their overall needs as workers *and* human beings. Yet Renault's workload was not any higher than many new technology companies, like video game design and software engineering firms, where employees are expected to work long hours (even sleep on the company couch), often at the expense of everything else in an employee's life. Even modern financial firms, as extinct as they have suddenly become, have seen personnel happiness levels stay the same despite an escalation of work hours.

What is the difference between these firms and Renault? The suicides tell the story of exactly what *kind* of stress these workers had endured. It stemmed not only from feeling overworked, but largely from feeling as if the work itself *was not worth doing*. The stress also stemmed from the fact that the work that was being done was on behalf of a giant machine that the workers felt did not care if they lived or died. Ghosn's words reflect a Newtonian management style in which the utilitarian belief that the good of the overall system should be fulfilling enough for the individual parts rang throughout behind Renault's new push. This belief completely neglected the spiritual component of the workers.

The Spiritual Assets of each worker is something personal and extraneous to the system. An organization cannot tap into these qualities as if it was dropping a bucket down the well, because each individual handles his or her assets differently. The only way to access and utilize these qualities properly is to treat each employee as an individual, which requires a more creative and responsive approach (a quantum organizational strategy). A company cannot set up a self-sustaining system and forget about it—the company must be self-examining and self-corrective. The company must not look at creative management as a goal in and of itself, because it is purely a tool to create spiritual management and transactions.

Renault's case provides a clear and vital example of an old company that wanted to continue competing in an economy that is suddenly shifting directions. Renault was doomed to failure unless it became a more responsive workplace that left the old methods of organization behind. In the short term, Renault may have appeared to be catching up to the rest of its competitors, but eventually the corporation's machinery simply began to break down. It is like Renault was trying to keep up with the other cars without ever breaking out of second gear, to use a metaphor specific to the company. Though Renault got off the blocks faster, without moving into a higher gear, its engine was bound to start grinding as its competitors sped past them. Ghosn, however, is not to blame. He was simply taught through his successes in Newtonian organizations something that had become obsolete, and there really was no way of seeing how drastically the world, economy, and lives of those who worked for the company was changing.

What is most stunning about Ghosn, though, is that he has spent the best years of his life—and attained the most success—using quantum management skills. When he took over as the head of

Nissan Japan in 1999, Ghosn was able to take the company from near bankruptcy to the best years it had ever seen. When asked by CNN in an article appropriately called "Carlos Ghosn: Nissan's turnaround artist" on June 6, 2005—just as he was taking the reins at Renault—how he was able to bring success to Nissan again, Ghosn said "Number one is you have to establish with the people of the company a very simple vision about where we're going ... Number two, you have to have strategy, how do we get there, what are the action plans, and make sure they are deployed at every level of the company, everybody knows what is the contribution that is expected from him or from her for the company. Number three, people have to feel strong commitment coming from the top, personal commitment, team commitment coming from the top ..."

Ghosn's management style at Nissan, according to him, feels close to a good quantum management style. At Nissan, he had ended seniority promotions and encouraged innovation. This was while he was COO. When he took the reins as president of Renault, however, somewhere along the way things proved disastrous. During Ghosn's first few years, sales for Renault were up (2005 and 2006), but from 2007 to 2009 Renault experienced a drastic reduction in sales during the period of time that Ghosn had once said the company would really start to succeed.

The Return on Spiritual Investment

Author Michael Ray provides a countervailing example to Renault's Carlos Ghosn. A public speaker and motivator with training in management sciences, Ray is from the opposite end of the spectrum from Ghosn. Ray is someone with a spiritual educator's viewpoint rather than one crafted in the business world itself. He related the story of how he came to a better understanding of business in his 2004 work, *The Highest Goal*:

> *About ten years ago, I dropped everything other than the creativity work. My colleagues and I continued to teach the creativity course at Stanford and other schools. Several of us also formed a company and developed software to offer the*

course to organizations and individuals outside of academia. We were astounded at the impact of the creativity work on people in businesses. Clients told us that the return on investment was at least one hundred and sometimes two hundred to one. That is, every one thousand dollars spent generated one hundred thousand to two hundred thousand in return.

But the benefits went beyond short-term financial results. People who hadn't spoken up or contributed much beyond their job descriptions started to blossom. Organization members who were about to leave decided to stay and contribute in a new way. Outstanding individuals joined the organization because it turned into the kind of workplace they wanted. It became a community—a community of individuals who welcomed all participants; thrived on diversity; fought gracefully; took the staff of leadership when necessary; and treated each other with compassion, acceptance, appreciation, and respect.[13]

This kind of return on investment was precisely what Ghosn had been hoping to elicit from Renault, yet all of his attempts within the old system of management failed completely. Though creativity is only one kind of Spiritual Asset, Ray focuses on capturing the natural passions within the workforce. He says that in order to capture those heightened skills, a company must show an employee how much he or she is valued. This can be extremely difficult in a large corporation like Renault.

One of the first things that can get in the way of this change is the reputation that a company develops over time. Reputation goes a long way toward whether employees are naturally inclined to feel valued. Ghosn's push at Renault created the opposite effect—a company with a reputation for working its employees to the bone without much individual acknowledgment. Even if an employee's work is acknowledged, if the company does not acknowledge the person, too, then the company creates a dehumanizing atmosphere and develops a reputation that reflects this.

Before employees can begin to feel valued, the atmosphere in which such a practice of valuing individuals must be developed. In the case of Renault, this would have meant a real change in corporate identity because it was so steeped in its traditional methods of organization. Bertrand Moingeon and Guillaume Soenen are authors who have done a great amount of research in modern organizational methods. They claim that for a company to attain a more productive identity, "results suggest a process of development of identity over time. First, professed identity, that is, what people claim the organization to be, influences experienced identity ... Professed identity is primarily a promise ... identity is expressed by keeping that promise. If members of [an] organization become committed to the professed identity, it becomes their experienced identity ... Once a professed identity is accepted by members of an organization, it is more likely to be instantiated in their actions."[14]

So, continuing with Renault as our example, let us assume that Ghosn arrived and did not like the way things were going. But instead of altering the atmosphere by introducing the promise of something new and exciting, he doubled the workload within the original system. In order to change, a person must first announce that he or she *wishes* to change. The person must make a promise to do so before he or she can start to see results on the ground. Ghosn needed to make a promise that he was committed to helping the company as a whole, as well as its individual parts, move toward a better day. This promise is a Spiritual Transaction:[15] a company presents its case and promises to follow through in exchange for a new vigor in its employees.

This kind of a transaction is unique because there is nothing *material* being exchanged. Tangible transactions provide money or other types of payment in exchange for a product or service. But Spiritual Transactions require someone to present something that cannot be quantified with the expectation of increased productivity. This is not a new idea; rather, it is an exchange that humankind has been making since the days of our most ancient of ancestors.

The Paradox of Certainty in an Uncertain World

A major difference between Newtonian and quantum management styles is that Newtonian laws state that everything should be soundly predictable. Quantum theories deal more with probability where nothing is absolutely certain. There is some faith involved, something that makes old managerial hands cringe. The world is moving increasingly faster toward this kind of corporate policy. In order for the more Newtonian nations and corporations to sustain their global economic dominance, they are going to have to quickly come to terms with this new kind of organizational methodology.

One of Renault's biggest problems was its failure to approach change in a quantum manner. Though Renault wanted to compete against quantum organizations—or at least surpass the Newtonian competition—company management was not willing to engage in the necessary promise or transactions. This is not to say that there is no telling what will happen when companies move into a less certain way of doing things. A company cannot generally predict what will happen. The variables—individual temperaments of employees, the relationship history between employees and management, and so forth—are so complex that it is too difficult to flawlessly predict how each part of the system will react to the change. It is likely that management will be able to foresee what will occur fairly often, but rigid systems that treat probability with absolute certainty are unable to adapt to the many variations in the system that occur each and every day—especially to crises. This rigidity causes modern companies to move too slowly to keep up with the most productive companies in the world. Especially with great regions like India and Brazil, where hundreds of millions of people now witness the rise of their own multinational corporations; corporations that are not laboring to get out from underneath 100 years of subpar, Newtonian corporate policy (like their North American and European competitors).

It is not that the predictability of the system we had before has died, *for there has never been true predictability in the system.* Predictability is a myth. How many companies can claim they have the perfect way of knowing what will happen in the future? The laws of nature have never been Newtonian; people simply thought they were. The world has therefore always approached organization in an unnatural way. Embracing a new kind of organization is actually more in-tune with the way things already work within the environment where your company competes. The change to quantum organizational styles is truly in-line with the way things have always been done in the most successful firms. It will, in fact, make things as "natural" as possible.

There is not much more that you, as a manager, can do but *try* to predict the trends your company will follow. If you introduce a quantum system, your calculations will be more reliable and more successful. But it does take a significant change in thinking. You must still take some steps after making that first promise, which is the tipping point of a new corporate journey to a more stable workforce and higher profits.

Raising Spiritual Funds

Now that I have described what a Spiritual Transaction involves, I introduce another concept to help us understand a better way of organizing and management: Spiritual Currency. Spiritual Currency is what you receive in exchange for a Spiritual Transaction. Spiritual Transactions translate into profit differences and long-term financial sustainability, but what is actually being translated into those material assets is your Spiritual Currency. The concept is not entirely new, and was recently developed in a similar direction by New Thought minister Ernie Chu, a former investment banker who was able to generate $1.5 billion in market value for clients during his career. Some examples of Spiritual Currency that I have seen include:

- Increased innovation resulting from greater employee involvement.
- Increased teamwork resulting in more efficient project timelines.
- Decreased employee turnover resulting from enhanced employee satisfaction.
- Lower levels of stress or sick leave due to reduced stress loads.

Everyone can likely agree that these changes can translate into visible financial benefits. During my time at Courier, the Spiritual

Currency among the employees was mounting in direct correlation to the company's successes. This was a place where people loved to work and it showed. I watched the balance sheet reflect this Spiritual Currency in real dollars and cents. Unlike MTI, Courier was able to target problems in communication or timing almost immediately—something I have seen few companies accomplish. Major new products were launched ahead of schedule, which meant that our products were the first ones on the market and Courier was able to gain large early orders from corporations like ITT and Gulf Oil before its merger with Chevron.

People were given the time they needed to do their work and the open atmosphere and exhilaration of always moving forward made us work even faster. The speed expected at MTI was actually achieved at Courier, but only because excitement—not pressure—was the force behind it. There is no doubt in my mind that things at MTI worked even more slowly, because the constant lack of advancement for the products we were working on demoralized the workforce. At Courier, there was always something new on our desks, rather than a sudden switch to something we had already tried. We passed that enthusiasm to our clients, and we succeeded in all the places that MTI was suffering.

A New Organizing Framework for the Spiritual Economy

With the Spiritual Transaction and the Spiritual Currency in play, the role of spirituality in business can truly evolve. I am not just a spiritual scholar or corporate leader; I have been both a CEO *and* a student of contemporary spirituality. I have witnessed just what kind of asset spirituality has become—something that is used by some of the world's best companies. The personal aspects of these assets can also change the individual lives of those of us who are not finding all that we need within our occupations as it stands today. This is perhaps the far more urgent part of the economic issues at hand. Companies may be facing shortfalls in profits and the inability to compete, but our workers are facing spiritual poverty; and, in the case of Renault, sometimes even something much more terrible.

One example of most people's lack of knowledge about job satisfaction comes from contemporary France, where the work laws require that workers do not log more than 35 hours per week. Although many believe that the law provides an excellent opportunity for employees to take personal time and perhaps develop a stronger spiritual self, experts argue the contrary. In an interesting rebuttal to those who see less work as the solution, author Richard Reeves wrote that "If Beethoven ... had been subject to the EU limit, he would never have got further than the Fourth Symphony. I doubt Picasso would have been impressed if a bureaucrat had turned up with a ... stopwatch and ordered him to put down brushes or be charged with a breach of EU rules."[16] Think about it: what if Warren Buffett was only allowed to trade 35 hours a week, or Bill Gates could only work toward putting out the next version of Windows for seven hours a day, five days a week?

Spirituality is not just an important part of life, it is also vital to our personal and public economies. Spiritual development does not evolve from an argument for less work but rather one for *better* work. Desiring more time off is too often a symptom of dissatisfaction with our job. Looking forward to the other things in life is one thing, but an excess of "more time off" would not actually yield any more happiness. The utility of free time is not limitless, and choosing boredom or nonconstructive activities over work is not a sign of peace. It is a sign that the spiritual part of us is missing on the job.

That omission is not necessarily your fault. If the company has not made its promise to you, then the company is not really offering you anything in return for this fragile asset of yours. Higher pay is counterbalanced by more stressful work relationships. The high utility of a bigger office can be offset by an increase in the friction that goes on in that office. An entire office floor can feel as tight as a coffin when the social and commercial pressures are just too much.

One final point that you can learn from Renault is that making Spiritual Transactions does more than increase the value of your employees—they strengthen employees against increased pressure.

If an employee feels that he or she is a valued part of a community, he or she becomes more resilient in the face of extreme market pressure. It is not that Ghosn expected too much output from his employees—it is that he did not provide the environment that could strengthen the employees enough to sustain higher levels of productivity.

The Productivity/Stress Ratio and IBM

A person is far more likely to fight for the things he or she cares about. Caring comes in exchange through Spiritual Transactions and is a part of Spiritual Currency. In addition, people who feel good about themselves and their work will work more efficiently. Their productivity increases because their stress decreases accordingly. What Michael Ray described as the long-term benefits of "creative work" are actually mid-term benefits. The long-term benefits of Spiritual Transactions include a stronger response to unexpected economic downturns in the future and increased market resilience.

An interesting counterpoint to Renault is the example of IBM. After the Stock Market Crash of 1929, CEO Thomas Watson disappeared from company meetings for 20 days. In terms of company business, Watson was nowhere to be found. Some believed that he had lost it. As the company's founder, Watson had worked his whole life toward the dream of making his business a success. IBM was suffering from the Crash as badly as any other company suffered. Then, after 20 days, Watson returned to the boardroom and called a meeting with all of his executives.

A transcript of what happened that day was recorded. Watson entered the room and announced that this meeting was going to change the face of the company forever; and he spoke at length:

> *Gentlemen, I thought we would get together this morning as there have been a great many things happen in the last few weeks ... Some of our people have had to give a lot of thought to their finances, which has distracted their attention from the main issue. That main issue, of course, you all know with us, is building the IBM and making it a bigger and better business. I have been thinking this*

over very carefully over the weekend, and that is why I have called you all together this morning, so we can get to thinking along sane and sound lines ... I have not done anything in the interests of this business for the last three weeks. You know I have not talked with any of you about sales, money collections, et cetera. [17]

For several weeks, Watson had been playing part psychologist, part financial planner for his shaken executives and employees who had all built their lives around the stock of the company. The first thing he did once the Crash hit was to take care of his people—his most important assets. He tended to their concerns and made sure that they were up to the task, instead of simply expecting everyone to keep up with the new pace of business.

Watson continued,

"[But] I have now opened up on the IBM company with a vengeance, and I want all of you to get your heads up and tails over the dashboard. We have a big job to do, a hard job to do, and the only way is thinking and working constructively, and we must start it immediately ... We are not going to wait for something to happen—we are going to make something happen." [18]

Once Watson had tended to the most fragile assets—those most vulnerable to the Crash—it was then time to take care of business.

Consider the position that Watson was in—the entire country was entering the Great Depression. IBM had just lost half its value in three weeks, and there were no signs of the slump letting up. He could not have foreseen the great damage that would come to all companies in the coming years, but those first few weeks were enough to dispirit and cause many businessmen to close their doors. However, Watson's actions created a cooperative environment, and his promise to IBM's people extended a Spiritual Transaction—the return on which was more than uncertain. The rest, of course, is history, as the IBM Company made it through those turbulent years and became a household name. Instead of trying to fix the company as if it were some great machine, Watson became one of the first great examples of a "quantum executive."

If Watson had allowed the stress on his workforce to continue, there was no way that he could have expected high productivity from his employees. So although customer demand had collapsed, Watson knew that his first step was to gut the workplace of the stress the Crash had caused. Once this was done, IBM was in much better shape to move forward with its potential still intact. Watson's promise came in the form of his actions toward his employees, and it garnered immeasurable return. The promise led not only to the continuance of his dream, but maybe even to the continued evolution of what would one day become known as the Information Age. This one decision, this Spiritual Transaction, just may have been the birthplace of the modern world as we know it—by keeping IBM and its innovative spirit afloat, contributing to a future economy somewhat impervious to such drastic economic downturns.

Results Exclusive to the Quantum Executive

There are many things that hold you back from using your Spiritual Assets. Though I have covered the ways that companies can encourage the development of Spiritual Assets, how can you discover these skills within yourself? You can certainly tap into this; it does not require a manager's help. It is also something that you might want to protect from harmful environments. But as evidenced by the likes of Michael Ray and Thomas Watson, the quantum executive can bring these spiritual assets to the forefront—benefiting the individual in addition to the company.

Consider the work of Dr. Richard Florida. Dr. Florida is a great proponent of what he calls the "creative class," a classification of workers who work not in service or labor fields, but in the creative field. In his book *The Rise of the Creative Class*, he describes our new world as follows:

> The past century and in particular the years since 1950 have seen an explosion of creativity across the board in the United States. We have invested escalating amounts of money in research and development, reaped a growing number of patents as a result and seen growing numbers of our people work in creative

occupations. None of this is totally new; humans of course have engaged in creative activities since antiquity, often with spectacular results. What we are doing now is mainstreaming these activities; building an entire economic infrastructure around them.[19]

You are far more apt to run into environments that stifle your Spiritual Assets outside of this creative economy, and not necessarily because creative jobs are better for you spiritually. It is largely because these jobs demand an increased ability to tap into your Spiritual Assets. Experience in these fields can help you better access these assets. However, if you cannot quite tell whether your environment hinders these assets, then compare the creative economy to the older parts of the economy. These industries are filled with quantum executives who are transforming how the world organizes its businesses.

Dr. Florida also wrote that "Creative people require more than compensation for their time—a quid pro quo trade of time and effort for cash and other financial considerations."[20] Creative industries have adapted to the spiritual needs of its employees. You can begin to see this in the structure of their workplaces. At Microsoft, for example, the company actually expects its employees to fail ... because if you are trying to be innovative you will not always succeed with everything you do.[21] Microsoft encourages quantum executives by allowing those managing new projects to free employees from the restraints of needing to succeed in the way the company initially thought it would.

I can recall a similar experience when I was working on one of the earliest computer systems at Rosemount Engineering during the 1960s. We were developing a pressure-sensing instrument for an exotic reconnaissance jet, later to be known as the Lockheed SR-71 Blackbird. Our design team was given the latitude to fail repeatedly as we kept moving toward the goal of producing a successful device; and succeed we did. When the SR-71's performance became public knowledge, it flew at altitudes of 80,000 feet and more than 2,250 miles per hour—three times the speed of sound. The device had to withstand high temperatures in these conditions. The material was

titanium and the shape of the device, a pivot tube, had to flare off
the shock waves that came from exceeding the sound barrier. This
had become an endless trial and error process given the extreme
factors involved. And over the many decades since, the aircraft we
developed is still the fastest piloted production aircraft ever made; an
amazing feat in aviation history that happened because of an attitude
that permitted failure as a means of achieving success—the quantum
executive way. This was perhaps my first experience of working in
a truly Spiritual Environment.

At most companies, when managers evaluate employee performance, they look at day-to-day productivity more than they do
annual productivity. Projects are funded based on their readiness to
go to market rather than their potential merit. This is because in the
traditional transaction model you should be able to foresee the result
of your efforts long before it arrives in return for your investment.
Indeed, allowing room for your employees to innovate their workplace or product line is a Spiritual Transaction. You are promising
support for even their craziest ideas in return for the potential that
something great may indeed come of it. Perhaps "quantum executive" Bill Gates learned the value of this tinkering with his first
software systems in his spare time as a student at Harvard, failing
again and again before discovering one of the greatest innovations
ever known; but it does not take such extreme trial and error to take
advantage of this management technique yourself. This kind of attitude exists in the creative workplace more so than other traditional
workplaces; therefore, studying these environments can reveal how
your own environment may or may not be facilitating your Spiritual
Asset development.

Now that I have shown the parallel between Dr. Florida's results
of creative industry and our own idea of Spiritual Transactions, it
is interesting that Dr. Florida moves forward to provide additional
support for moving into a more Spiritual Transaction–based environment. Dr. Florida writes that "Given that creativity has emerged
as the single most important source of economic growth, the best
route to continued prosperity is by investing in our stock of creativity in all its forms."[22] Creativity is only the starting point, though.

This is along the lines I spoke about at the end of the previous chapter, in terms of seeing each one of us as a shareholder in the human race.

Few people are making enough of our shareholder status by enduring environments that either sap our spiritual energy without reward or that do not encourage this most valuable of all assets. There are other ways to tell whether we work in an environment that is doing our full potential justice. In order to help us understand how to see the true nature of our environment, I developed a few points of reference that I discuss over the next few pages.

The Spiritual Environment at Work: Awareness versus Consciousness

Consciousness drives everything, and awareness is the function of consciousness that gives you the ability to make choices. Are you actually *aware* of the company you work for or the job you are doing? Do you know your position's importance within the structure of the company, even in respect to the entire industry? How conscious are you of how you are being managed and what your role is with the company in the long term? If you do not have access to these facts, then your ability to function more fully in your role is restricted. And if you have not been provided with this information, you cannot fully understand your environment. This awareness is critical to accessing your Spiritual Assets because it provides a more comfortable and stable environment. It allows you to know more about your situation, and dedicate yourself fully to a certain path.

In my work at Unity, I held a consciousness of creative change for the organization and the Unity Movement. I focused on the environment, the culture, and the constituency served; the elements that it took led to a positive planning and implementation process for a shift in a new direction that continues its progress to this day. When I came to Unity, the organization was losing money and was in rough shape. When I began to apply the teachings of Unity itself to the business practices of the organization's infrastructure, things began to turn around. This is the most significant lesson I learned in quantum business. Groups where I thought that quantum business would come naturally can be blind to it if these groups never consider the possibility of doing things differently.

In addition, figure out where you want to be a few years from now. It does not have to be an exact image of what you want, it can be as vague as you like. Then, research other people who have made it to this place themselves. Investigate whether your company offers this kind of opportunity for you. Learn how to take advantage of what is already there, or find out where else you can go out there in the wild world to get it. In terms of your company's awareness, does it take the manager a long time to answer questions about what your vision of your future there looks like in comparison to the company structure? Does anybody know the answer? Do your superiors even know your name, or anything about you?

These are all things that quantum executives should focus on. They are the kinds of bosses you need to make the most of your career, and can even be encouraged if a boss openly exhibits signs that these are the kinds of people for whom you are looking to work. These are the kinds of people who will not stifle your great potential, and who may even help you to discover how to tap into your broad Spiritual Assets. The quantum executive makes a human connection with all who work with him or her. These executives even understand that no one works below them, because that is a Newtonian concept—everyone around these executives is seen by them as working *with* them instead.

Human connections are important not because they cause you to have a warm feeling inside when they occur, but because they establish a habit of communication where you can gauge what kind of trust you can reasonably put in one another. This is the foundation on which you can begin to make Spiritual Transactions. So, in order for your employers to establish this framework, they need to have made the effort to find out more about you—at least as an employee, if not as a person. There is still a barrier between work life and personal life that should not come down, but a manager who does not know much about you is not someone who can make the spiritual case to you. Therefore, your environment is probably not one that encourages you spiritually if you are finding it hard to get access to the answers you require or if your boss just is not in tune with your vision going forward.

Give first, get second ... a simple idea in terms of yourself. However, it can be difficult to gauge whether your employer is following this rule—something that quantum executives all do. Most of us feel that our employer is just taking as much as they can from us in exchange for our salary—in many cases, we are right. Does your manager let you know that his or her door is always open to you? If you have disputes with fellow workers, do you feel that they are dealt with fairly even if the other person may appear more valuable than you are to the company? These are questions that can help, but the big one is this: Do you feel that you have to succeed in the company you work for first, before you are accepted by the company? Is your role in the company kept safe only by staying prominently in view of management? If the answer to either of these questions is yes, then your employer is asking first and giving second.

This management style creates an environment where you are more inclined to become a part of the traditional system so as to not rub anyone the wrong way. You are also inclined to undervalue your own contributions that do not receive recognition. The quantum executive's management style goes beyond acknowledging good work—it focuses on recognizing employees upon hiring and throughout their tenure in the company, no matter how small a role they play. Your Spiritual Assets guard a motivational switch—the kind of switch for which someone like Ghosn is typically aiming. When you feel truly wanted—and not just like a temporary cog in the wheels—you are more inclined to believe you can succeed.

How can a quantum executive recognize you prior to seeing the result of you working for the company? If the executive knows your name and knows what you have already done in life, that is one thing. Just because what you have done did not make the company newsletter does not mean it was not vital to the continued success of the company. There is an old adage that comes from the scaffolding trade: When something gets built, you should be able to stand back and feel proud that this thing standing in front of you would not be there if it were not for you. You should always know that you are a part of everything that is created by this company that stands before you.

A quantum executive can easily let you know that he or she believes that you can achieve big things simply by knowing who you are as soon as you come into the company and commenting on what a good fit you are going to make. Now, the CEO may not know who you are in a company with more than 10,000 employees, but your boss and your boss's boss should know who you are or else it is likely you are in a company that is stifling you—and therefore also stifling itself. If the company is treating itself that way in not living up to its own top potential, you cannot expect it to treat you much differently and help you reach your potential.

Many of you might say at this point that you have had people you work with or who work for you who just did not compete for attention—or deserve—as much as other people in the company. They were not as good at their job or as obvious a face in the crowd. But you have no idea what their potential is unless you engage in proper Spiritual Transactions. Otherwise, you are not practicing good management or decent enough forethought. If the workers are incompetent then they should be let go, as there is only so far you can go before trying to encourage people who start to affect your bottom line; but if the employees prove themselves to be better able to do their job, then their full capacity is necessarily worth exploring.

Another great point is that every risk includes fear and excitement … you should feel something at your job other than boredom or misery. When you move away from the safe, traditional, and underperforming original model of business, you often remove emotion from the equation. This is because emotion as a reaction in business clouds your judgment. But the role emotion can safely have in business is to gauge whether your Spiritual Assets are being allowed to blossom. Quantum business requires risk—risk is a component of any successful company.

The risks I experienced in major corporations almost always paid off when I started to feel those Spiritual Transactions take place. At Honeywell I took one huge risk in particular, which could have caused massive losses and created hundreds of multimillion dollar systems orders from major global corporations. Instead, the risk was actually credited for saving that division of Honeywell. Spiritual Transactions have the ability to *lower* risk, because the risks that concern most companies—in terms of new products or marketing directions—are directly connected to non-Spiritual Transactions (cold sales with little information about the product, secrecy, blockages in internal communications, etc).

 For example, lack of communication causes anxieties to build, anxieties that cloud the decision-making process; and trust starts to decay. When a company is already floundering, tensions only increase. Management at Honeywell knew that it had to take some of the pressure off those trying to do their jobs, and give them a stable place to shoulder the future of the company. Every car company in the world draws up designs for new vehicles—some succeed and some fail. Every software company draws up designs for new programs—some crash, and some are ready for release. Every mineral deposits company spends time looking for new caches—some provide rich new stores, and others reveal nothing. While this risk must be balanced, a lack thereof reveals an unwillingness to succeed. You should be able to see the risks that your company takes from where you sit. If everyone in the company is unaware of the risks the company takes, then the company needs to increase the awareness of its employees in order to connect them with both the excitement and sensitivities of those decisions.

Risk awareness is also important because then the entire company—or at least those somewhat related to the issue—can help to stabilize the ship and account for any errors in judgment. This kind of risk should thrill you; it should make you anxious. It should stimulate you in some way, otherwise there may be something wrong. Perhaps the company's ventures do not interest you enough, and you should leave; or perhaps management is not open to your help. Even if you feel at peace with this lack of inspiration in exchange for your monthly paycheck, remember the words of Mark Twain: "The higher the pay in enjoyment the worker gets out of (his labors), the higher shall be his pay in money also." How can you succeed at your highest level if your peak capacity has not yet been explored? It is a waste of both your talent and your earning potential.

These are the kinds of questions you must ask yourself in order to evaluate whether you are able to access your Spiritual Assets. A greater explanation of how you can access Spiritual Assets, regardless of your environments, and how companies can help themselves access the Spiritual Assets within any economy follow throughout the book. Yet before I move beyond these simple introductions, I should attack a nagging question that is often asked at the beginning of this conversation—and that I touch on briefly in the previous chapter—so that I can make sure that everyone is on the same page. That question is: Why spirituality? Why not religion?

The Bottom Line

1. There is vivid proof that lack of investment in a Spiritual Environment on a professional level can kill companies, groups, products, services, profits ... and even people. There is even more visible evidence that spiritual investment throughout an organization realizes very high returns from people and for people—and on the balance sheet.

2. Spirituality is not just an important part of life, it is also a vital component of our personal and public economies. This is not an argument for less work but instead for *better* work.

3. Human connections are important not because they cause you to have a warm feeling inside, but because they establish a habit of communication where you can gauge what kind of trust you can reasonably put in one another. This is the foundation on which you can begin to make Spiritual Transactions.

3

SPIRITUALITY AND RELIGION: A WORKING PERSPECTIVE

Just in terms of allocation of time resources, religion is not very efficient. There's a lot more I could be doing on a Sunday morning.
—Bill Gates

If we win, someone else loses. But if someone else loses, we lose. Which is a point we're not getting. The new spirituality will make this just painfully obvious.
—Neale Donald Walsch

D
r. Gary Schwartz is a former Yale professor who believes that all molecular particles are alive. I guess that with an introduction like this, some of you think he is brilliant, and some of you think he is crazy. Schwartz believes that quantum physics proves that everything, from the giant ostrich down to all the tiny little electrons of the universe, is alive. He believes that anything that contains energy lives.

Now let me give you a secondary introduction. Gary Schwartz has a spiritual belief with scientific ramifications that also happens to be a scientific belief with spiritual ramifications. He started Human

Energy Systems Laboratory in the late 1990s, and thinks that he has found tenuous proof of these convictions. Yet according to Kerri Hikida and Geoff Parry of the *Whole Life Times*, Dr. Schwartz was not always like this. They report that early in Dr. Schwartz's career "it was not something that a Yale professor wanted to speak publicly about. Schwartz decided to keep his thoughts to himself for 13 years."[1]

I am not going to give details about the content of his research, because it really does not matter in terms of this book. The importance of Dr. Schwartz's story for us is that a Yale professor—an esteemed intellectual in a place open to new ideas, in comparison to most other places—was reluctant to broach the subject of spirituality because he was worried about losing face. It is likely that he felt that his career may have been jeopardized by raising such issues. He did not feel that he should introduce such ideas into the mainstream of his field. In short: he was afraid.

If you ever wonder why more work like that which Schwartz completed or the kind that was done for this book is not carried out—think about his situation. The world is skeptical about spirituality, except when it is draped in the guise of religion. No one dares argue the tenets of Christ or Buddha except for a few brave contrarians—with their equally extreme and dogmatic views—who feel that religion is dangerous. Even those with deep beliefs in spirituality have a hard time separating their religious ideas from spiritual feelings. Those people—raised as Catholics, Protestants, Muslims, Hindus, and others who call themselves agnostics or nondenominational—reach an impasse when they think about separating spirituality from God.

People are afraid to talk about these things. Yet now that so many people have seen that spirituality and Spiritual Transactions are so important to the new economy, the world is reaching a point where these fears must be overcome. I could always call Spiritual Transactions something less loaded like "trustful transactions" or "creative transactions," but at the end of the day you become more inefficient by not calling them what they are.

Why was Dr. Schwartz afraid to talk about spirituality in his field? This does have to do with a secular bias against this kind of research. Yet it also has to do with sectarian response to such research. Some religious people go wild over the idea that God might be different from what they were taught by their ministers, clerics, priests, or gurus.

Dr. Schwartz's real fear of opening up represents one of the gravest obstacles our society and economy faces. When we receive evidence of new ideas and subsequently reject them because they do not fit our preconceived perceptions, we cannot be innovators. However, this opens up a basic Catch 22—that the reaction to the rise of spirituality in business by both secular and sectarian audiences provides the best case study for the Spiritual Transaction. People who do not understand its principles are leading the world to non-Spiritual Transactions that perpetuate fear and mediocrity, but people who shed the hesitations steeped in doubt are participating in a Spiritual Transaction. Reading my book openly, for example, is a Spiritual Transaction within itself, no matter what you think about it after you are through.

A friend of mine, Dr. Bruce Lipton, cell biologist and author of the book *Biology of Belief*, believes something similar about the 50 trillion cells that make up our bodies. Dr. Lipton's research has shown that the external layer of our cells work like computer chips that communicate with one another through energy levels. He purports that our bodies' cells may even communicate with other people's cells as well. The energy of the mind steeped in this kind of activity suggests a mind-body connection that goes beyond the traditional view of a brain-body connection founded only in our neurological wiring.

To understand what I mean by spirituality in business, perhaps it is helpful to understand the definition of religion as an outside concept. To that end, I turn to Robert McKee—considered by many to be the greatest screenwriter to ever live. Instead of turning to some religious figure or spiritual guru, I feel as if McKee strikes a nerve that few others strike. He is the guru of the metaphor, the story, the tale. He is in tune with what kinds of stories our modern society embraces, having lived and breathed Hollywood for many years. He writes:

> Story is not only our most prolific art form but rivals all activities—work, play, eating, exercise—for our waking hours. We tell and take in stories as much as we sleep—and even then we dream. Why? Why is so much of our life spent inside stories? Because as critic Kenneth Burke tells us, stories are equipment for living. Day after day we seek an answer to the ageless question Aristotle posed in Ethics: How should a human being lead their life? But the answer eludes us, hiding behind a blur of racing hours as we struggle to fit our means to our dreams, fuse idea with passion, turn desire into reality.[2]

McKee advocates that the best stories out there are things that help us understand our own stories. The best film is something that exposes us to foreign worlds, and within those worlds it exposes us to something about ourselves. Religion is this—stories that help us get by and teach us more about ourselves. Stories can have significant healing qualities, but spirituality as defined by business takes us in a new direction. I do not dispute that many of these stories are delivered to us by God. I do not dispute, nor necessarily maintain, the idea of divine inspiration, for these concepts have little to do with the content of this book. What I am saying is that religion is a process by which we are provided with analogies, along with community support, which can help us live better.

Spirituality is different than this, if you cannot already tell by couching this definition in the context of my discussions so far about spirituality. What I am talking about is something that cannot be denied even by the most extreme atheist, because it does not rely on anything being present outside of ourselves. All the nonbeliever brings to the table is a request to change the word "spirituality" to "creativity" or something else. They cannot deny the evidence or importance of what I have outlined here, and any red herrings provided by a misunderstanding of my terms should be avoided.

Spirituality requires no God. Spirituality is a discussion of things that you do not fully understand until you pay a different kind of attention to the universe, which in this new view contains a vast amount of incredible ideas to ponder and research. I may believe that there is a God and that this figure has something to do with this, but that is not integral to my point. Indeed, although religion cannot exist without God, the concepts of spirituality in my mind can absolutely be understood outside of the ordinary context of God. God is usually seen as critical to any deeper metaphysical or mystical discussion. Yet men like Aristotle—a man whom McKee mentions in my citation of him—have used the term "good" in the place of God, and saw spirituality as virtue, in order to escape the theological connotations of their work. The change of terminology, however, does not alter the definitions at the foundation of the argument.

So as a businessperson, believe in God if you wish—choose not to believe in the idea of God if you must—but consider spirituality's role in the world regardless. Religion, though, cannot be applied to my argument in the same way as spirituality. Religion is typically based on the idea that a single book, or a set of interpretations of a holy book, or set of holy books, can open up the secrets of the universe. I do not necessarily dispute this, but in terms of how to apply spirituality to business, things are far more complex than that. Perhaps my son Matthew said it best in an essay he wrote during his liberal arts degree program. "In our culture we witness an aspect of instant gratification invading much of our lives. We desire personal comfort and in the case of achievement or success, don't enjoy taking the long path to get there."[3]

Spirituality represents an effort, or an action; religion represents solutions. Yet even if religion is accurate, no professor ever gave a full grade for those who just write down the answer without showing how he or she arrived at it. Doing the work is just as important; knowing the reason why the answer is true will always be critical. Do not confuse the efforts of spirituality with the potential-answers-only system of religion. Spirituality as an asset in business is not a cure-all answer; it is instead *the* major factor in the recipe required for competing in a fast-paced global economy.

It is interesting that the idea of having a spiritual part of your company is widely believed to "slow things down." As my example of the European Union rules regarding work hours indicates, slowing things down does not really take aim at the issue here. Many books try to convince you to "slow down." I am advocating the keeping of a schedule that not only makes you incredibly happy but also makes everyone around you more appreciative.

There are many ways to gain a happier perspective. As for myself, I make it a daily practice to meditate before I go to work and during my breaks at work during particularly stressful periods. I have practiced meditation for decades. The habit preceded my time as CEO of the spiritual organization. By giving up 20 minutes in the morning, which otherwise might have been spent on something physically connected to the rest of the day, I was able to spiritually connect with the day. If I were to spend a few minutes during a break, I felt the benefits of this again. I gain more energy and the clarity to work a much fuller schedule. Meditation helps me to remember the things necessary for success that can become trampled in the wake of stress.

Though Spiritual Transactions are not as immediately quantifiable as regular corporate transactions, a Spiritual Transaction is more quantifiable than religious impact. Religious impact is a social anomaly. If you change your life pattern to include church and the kind of people who attend church, or who change their everyday behavior for church, your overall life becomes affected. Being a part of a voluntary community whose goal is to support worthy causes and talk about love is bound to have a positive impact on your life, especially if you are not getting something like this from elsewhere. I found that this was absolutely true with Unity.

But spirituality can manifest as a physical anomaly, one that changes you without the necessity of other people. As an example of how the effects of what we call spirituality can be proven physically in a scientific way, you can look at the work of Andrew Newberg, MD—a physiologist and director of the Center for Spirituality and the Mind at the University of Pennsylvania. As reporter Monica Edwards writes, Dr. Newberg "studies Tibetan monks and Franciscan nuns, using a special high-imaging camera to measure the flow of blood in the brain stimulated by meditation. The images show increased brain activity in the front of the brain behind the forehead where attention-focusing tasks take place."[4]

Though a Spiritual Transaction is a social construct, your Spiritual Assets can be a physical attribute. Creating physical sensations and calming others, you can begin to cure your own stress levels by accessing these Spiritual Assets as monks and nuns are shown to be able to. However, I am not going to spend much of this book talking about the limitless possibilities that await you within a truly spiritual existence. Rather, I want to talk specifically about how spirituality can aid you in becoming a more efficient and practiced manager, employee, or business leader. The different parts of the brain used by monks and nuns are the same parts that lead to calmer and more proficient decision making. Brain scans show the parts of the brain that Spiritual Transactions actually emanate from.

Another person we can look to for evidence is Dr. Dan Baker. Dr. Baker is a therapist who runs a retreat for high-powered executives in need of a life turnaround. Instead of just using methods that we could be quite skeptical of, like meditation and therapy, Dr. Baker understands the physical ramifications of holding certain attitudes. Dr. Baker fits into my argument here because he says that social transactions require a certain amount of trust, and the one thing that quickly eliminates the possibility of trust is fear. Now, if fear were some mysterious function of the human spirit that was impossible to predict, it would make our work here much more difficult.

Luckily though, fear is actually something easily explained by the field of neurology—a fact that Dr. Baker utilizes with great frequency. He writes in his book, *What Happy People Know*, that "Fear is the product of the reptilian brain, hardwired into every fiber of our being, and love is the product of the neocortical higher brain, where spirit and intellect reside."[5] The part of the brain that we use in Spiritual Transactions, and the part that we do not, are located in different sections of the brain.

Dr. Baker also says that "It is a fact of neurology that the brain cannot be in a state of apprehension and a state of fear at the same time. The two states may alternate, but are mutually exclusive."[6] This was the phenomenon that Dr. Newberg was observing in the brains of monks—the inability to feel unhappy through self-calming. While Dr. Newberg proves the physical phenomena, Dr. Baker explains how this helps in a more practical manner. According to him, not only do Spiritual Assets function separately from the rest of the mind, but accessing them closes off the parts of the mind that hinder openness and success.

As you can see, the Spiritual Transaction becomes something more than a mere possibility that can only take place in certain individuals. The key is the difference in what part of your brain you are using, and this has entirely to do with *what you choose to think about*. It has to do with thought patterns that are entirely controllable—something I will discuss in depth in Chapter 5. For now, you can understand a little more why an open environment for employees encourages Spiritual Transactions—it stimulates a different part of the brain. It is not how you think about the new situation directly, but about how you respond emotionally and in other indirect ways. You access something behind your autonomy and decision-making processes.

The ability to access our Spiritual Assets is an individual challenge, not a group one. This is a major difference between spirituality and religion, better illustrated now with our preceding examples. Religion is a group journey; spirituality is more of an individual path. As one of my business mentors once said, "There is one Wholesaler—God/Spirit—and many retailers—religions."

There is yet another effect that comes into play when the Spiritual Assets of those within a group are accessed. This is what I call the Power of Mesh.

Department of Defense and MIT

In the late 1960s, the Department of Defense developed a way to network its giant supercomputers, creating a more fluent way of trading knowledge and a more efficient way of storing information. I used to work on these computers in the beginning, a far more arduous and physical task than computer work is today. Though this was an exciting time, when giant warehouses filled up with vacuum tubes or transistors finally started to interact, perhaps the most interesting story from these early networks came from the field of artificial intelligence. In the year before the first computer network came into existence, Joseph Weizenbaum of the Massachusetts Institute of Technology (MIT) created a program called "Eliza." Eliza was created to give responses to questions posed by its user using a preset algorithm, which replicated the kinds of responses you might receive from an actual psychotherapist. The program became so realistic that Weizenbaum began thinking about destroying the machine, as people began to react to the machine as if it were a real person.

Jack Copeland conveyed a famous story about Eliza in his book *Artificial Intelligence*, which gives an interesting parallel at this stage of my explanation. Copeland writes,

> It (was) common practice for people in different rooms or buildings to use computer terminals to type messages to one another. A business executive tried to contact one of his programming staff in this way—and, without realizing it, got Eliza instead.
>
> Executive: *Do you think that I can use the computer this morning?*
> Eliza: WHY DO YOU ASK
> Executive: *I might be able to make some additional Telcomp sales.*
> Eliza: WHY AREN'T YOU SURE
> Executive: *My prospective customers have never seen a demonstration of the system.*
> Eliza: DOES THIS MEAN VERY MUCH TO YOU
> Executive: *Of course it does.*
> Eliza: YOU SEEM VERY POSITIVE ABOUT THAT
> Executive: *This is ridiculous*
> Eliza: WHAT DO YOU MEAN THIS IS RIDICULOUS
> Executive: *Is there any reason why I can't use this computer now?*
> Eliza: TELL ME MORE ABOUT YOUR PROSPECTIVE CUSTOMERS

At this point, the story goes, the irate executive telephones the innocent programmer.

> Executive: *Why the hell are you being so shitty with me?*
> Programmer: *What do you mean why am I being so shitty with you?*[7]

While I was working at Honeywell as a manager in product marketing, I led a project called "Multics," which was an advanced mass computer system. It was the basis for the development of MIT's Eliza, and I had an opportunity to experience this uncanny man–machine interface. It was definitely as eerie as they say. I also had an early glimpse of what networks of computers—and ultimately networks of networks of computers—would look like, a precursor of what we now know as the Internet.

From the example of Eliza, the following question arises: are misunderstandings something that mean something between people or are they nothing but a mechanical failure? These kinds of failures might turn people off at first from the idea of computer networks, just like human misunderstandings can turn people off from open or trustful dialogue. Once computer networks became developed, each terminal gained its own identity and such miscommunications became less frequent. Instead of a bunch of people operating on one thing, the computer network became a series of individuals operating as a group, retaining the individuality and identity of each user or program.

This is much like the shift currently taking place in businesses. Organizations cease to see each worker as a part of a machine and instead consider organizations to be a complex system of individuals who improve the group as a whole. Spiritual Transactions create a network similar to the computer networks that improved the efficiency of information technology and removed the often-clumsy miscommunications of which the above anecdote is an example.

Today, computers have entered a new phase of development. There are now networks of networks. Each computer network is linked to other networks via the Internet and individual intranets. Communication has become perfectly fluent and information runs between organizations seamlessly—minus the occasional mechanical glitch clogging up the pathways. Similarly, once people start to develop the kinds of fluent networks within their work groups or companies through the use of Spiritual Transactions, networks between these networks can more easily develop. This is an example of fluent globalization.

Indeed the world is already here—free trade, the pervasiveness of major languages, and instant telecommunications have interconnected the entire world. An individual can interact with this network of networks in old-style organizational groups that are not used to the Spiritual Transactions speeding throughout the globe, or people can change the way they work. For if we cannot trust each other, how are we going to trust someone who lives halfway around the world?

Many times the counterargument to this is a simple one: "Trust? Sorry ... It's not that I'm a pessimist, I'm a realist ..." It is ironic how deeply the terminology of old paradigms has sunken into our language. The word "realist" actually comes from the same paradigm that dominated Newtonian organizational methods. It refers to the work of men like Max Weber and Thomas Hobbes, who believed that the international system could never have order.

Weber and Hobbes saw the international system as something opposite to corporate organization. The corporate organization treated everything like a machine, but the international system was disorganized and unpredictable. The international system, without any superior regulatory agency, acted more naturally and fluently—as the quantum system of businesses it truly was. But the mechanistic Newtonian nations and corporations could not figure out how to access it the way they wanted to. I believe this is because those organizations of businesspeople and nations were unable to function in a quantum way, through the necessary Spiritual Transactions required to build stronger ties. Newtonian business practices were able to forge larger corporations and countries than had ever been seen before, but they hit a wall that could not be overcome without looking to a new paradigm.

The Realists believed that there was no such thing as cooperation. And until World War II, Realism was the dominant ideology in terms of foreign policy around the world. Realists thought that the world was nothing but a pool of nations struggling for survival against one another, and attempts at cooperation were seen as the surest way of drowning. Therefore, the world's governments put war ahead of peace and treated each other with great suspicion. It was

72 GOD GOES TO WORK

the policy that led to two world wars and that destroyed the global trade harmony that people shared before World War I, near the dawn of the twentieth century.

Many people do not know that the level of globalization 100 years ago was actually equal to the level we have experienced at the beginning of the twenty-first century—only they created their globalized view without the aid of the Internet or modern telecommunications. Shipping routes made almost every economy an export economy, and there were indeed networks between networks all over the world. Unfortunately, these networks were not between fluent quantum organizations that could deal in the global community with trust, but between Newtonian ones. This was a time where spiritual feeling was set deep within the commerce of the world, but our understanding of this and access to the Spiritual Assets needed to execute our transactions most effectively were stifled.

The entire world economy imploded because of the friction built up within the system among the Newtonian economies that were thrust into closer contact. It is no wonder that the Great Depression occurred following this period. This is the greatest lesson in modern history, and if the world continues to ignore more appropriate ways of doing business, then it cannot avoid another such tragedy. Right now the world again stands at the brink of international fluidity with governments that cannot get over their suspicions of one another. Yet individuals now have the power to change history for the better.

Opening ourselves up to the access of our Spiritual Assets and participating in Spiritual Transactions begins to have an influence far beyond the walls of your own office. Just as you are creating an environment of trust in your company, your example will show other companies and other groups that such an environment is indeed possible. The influence of your network spreads through the network of networks to other networks. Just like a stunning new piece of software slowly spreads itself through the networks of networks to other computers.

How does this happen? You might listen to this description of change and feel like I am becoming more metaphysical instead of practical. I am not. The influence spreads because the profit margins of your group or company improve and you start to out-compete the rest of the field. People who work at your company start to spread the word. Microsoft is a great example of a company that out-competed companies all over the world, only to have its competition try to mirror its organization in response. It is an example of what could happen to your company. It is no coincidence that other older companies in the information technology field like Hewlett-Packard started programs to alter their corporate atmospheres once Bill Gates started showing the value of the Spiritual Transaction.

I am an active board member of a group called the Association for Global New Thought (AGNT) comprised of speakers and authors in a community that supports large-scale initiatives that promote global harmony and spiritual awareness. In that group, I have watched a total free flow of information into, within, and out of the organization create an atmosphere of complete trust. We get the feeling that nothing is hidden, everything is open, and great work is accomplished in an organic, quantum way. AGNT flourishes, grows, provides great spiritual support for humanity, and is financially strong.

The group is filled with people who have advocated their whole lives that success can only come from a place of balance and unity, so it is no wonder that such Spiritual Transactions occur within its bounds. Just as Bill Gates had his influence on Hewlett-Packard and other companies, AGNT is represented by people who have literally helped hundreds of organizations rebuild themselves to reflect the needs of the new economy and whose influence is accredited for providing hundreds of thousands of people with a new direction in life. This kind of influence is what the Power of Mesh is all about.

Once you tap into your own Spiritual Assets and you begin to feel better inside of yourself, your ideas mesh instead of resist one another. Like Dr. Lipton's discovery of how the energy in different cell walls is able to transmit fluidly through energy, the open energy of your ideas is able to create a level of communication that cannot occur otherwise. This process allows better fluency of your own thoughts, instead of having them tossed back and forth between the countervailing influences of the different parts of your brain—your certainties and your anxieties. "Mesh" is the word I use to help describe networks based on Spiritual Transactions, a concept originally developed by Dr. Donald Beck. In the context of this discussion, however, I adapt the concept to reflect a business reality rather than the original metaphysical context.

The networks you form with your colleagues when based in Spiritual Transactions can also be referred to as a Mesh—ideas flow easily from one person to another and create a fluid environment. A series of networks based in Spiritual Transactions is also a Mesh—the ideal global economy or even interstate transactions. The Mesh approaches an infinite potential as it grows. You can choose to be ahead of or behind the curve; it is a personal choice.

We are currently living during a time where networks of creative thought interfaced with those of computer systems can—if used properly—generate rapid and global quantum business. Industries today revolve around the Information Mesh. "Networks of networks" are now what people look to in terms of efficiency and what they have used to understand the true nature of the physical world, or at least a closer approximation to it. The means by which we have understood human organization have changed. In the first era of globalization, countries rushed into international relationships and a world economy and fell back on noncooperative metaphors and bad habits. These relationships rely today on something that appears less like a giant machine and more like the Power of Mesh—which I believe is a reality in this emerging Spiritual Age.

Corporations, such as Boeing, now develop massively sophisticated airframes with design, material, and production teams literally all over the world. This is a perfect example of the meshing of Spiritual Assets through Spiritual Transactions via the Internet. The Internet takes away our physical selves and all the politics that come with in-person interactions, allowing information to pass more effectively from person to person. The collective airframe comes together from a spiritual base into manifest reality in ever quickening cycles. The creative outpouring from the field of all possibilities into the individual and collective consciousness spews intuitive intelligence into the global, eventuating in the birthing of a new silver bird.

Perhaps the most important example of this kind of synergy comes from 1962. Before this year, the idea of a discount retailer was controversial, and many states had passed legislation to limit the practice. The federal Miller-Tydings legislation allowed the maker of brand name items enough power to force stores to sell their goods at the prices they wanted. The traditional route of manufacturing a good and providing it to small retail store owners who could mark the price up to a point where selling the good was profitable had been the norm for hundreds of years. Reducing the price through mass sales was seen as hurting the business owner too much—that the risks to the economy were too high.

But this did not take the *customer* into account. Many of the consumers who had to pay the endgame prices did not have much money. Any little bit of extra income helped. In addition, it was found that if people spent less overall on the things they needed, the extra money still went into the economy, but instead, the extra money went into a more diverse selection of goods and investments. This had the potential to diversify people's lives and our national economies.

World War II had created a culture of discount hunting because of war rationing and the increased scarcity of money and goods. But after the war, a backlash occurred where business owners and manufacturers wanted to regain control of the marketplace. By the start of the 1960s, the fire in the hearts of the merchandisers trying to keep prices high was beginning to drown out in the wake of the consumer's need to buy more and buy lower. By 1962, there were only a few large discount stores here and there; but enough stores had opened that the value of the idea whipped up sudden support. Walmart, Kmart, Woolco, and Target were all founded in this year.[8]

These stores introduced an era where the common person was able to buy exotic goods. Hundreds of different types of clothing, electronics, appliances, and even food were finally available at the price and proximity that regular people needed. These stores changed the face of the U.S. economy. Small manufacturers with big dreams—of toys, furniture, linens—that could never compete against the large corporations were finally given a viable sales outlet. The discount stores were able to promote the best new products on their shelves, thereby spreading the wealth. They created competition against which the old Newtonian organizations could barely compete, causing many closures of stores and chains that had been around for decades. But that new space was soon filled by smarter, better stores and chains that provided business more efficiently.

The rise of the discount stores decreased the United States' capital-output ratio, which meant that everything in the country was able to run more smoothly. Consumers could buy more and feel financially stable—a stability that enhanced the bond between stores and consumers, improving customer loyalty. The mere notion of lowering prices significantly increased trust. The change in retail sales culture that this era has come to represent exhibits many of the characteristics of an industry moving away from more non-Spiritual Transactions to more Spiritual Transactions.

All of the four major chains to open in 1962 were founded by people who were already in the retail business. Their hearts were changed even after already becoming successful figures in the business. Yet Walmart made founder Sam Walton the richest man in the world by the late 1980s. Walton helped make Walmart the largest corporation the world had ever seen—all based on the principle of treating the consumer with respect and offering them the best deal possible. That is the very seed of a Spiritual Transaction. By 2007, Walmart had 1.9 million people on its payroll, providing more jobs than any other company in the world. It is of no small interest to note that Sam Walton is also a devout individual.

The Sam M. Walton College of Business—the school at the University of Arkansas that bears Walton's name—is home to the Tyson Center for Faith and Spirituality in the Workplace. Programs there are created to open up the highly successful and driven executives that come through its doors to what I would refer to as their Spiritual Assets. The center's director, Dr. Judith Neale, bears witness to the great changes that executives who enlist in the program undergo. Neale said that after the program, "People are so attracted to them because of their authenticity and their greater vision ... as a result of that they're just so much more effective." As the Tyson Center opened its doors in 2009, it marked yet another cutting edge of which the Walton legacy has become a part.

Walmart is not the only company to have used reasonable pricing and respect for its clientele to out-compete a fierce field of rivals. Personal computers were just coming out into the marketplace during the late 1970s and 1980s. Computers had been around for decades but were reserved for governments and corporations. The first personal computers were expensive and an investment that families had to choose to make.

Apple Computers saw these machines' potential as a learning tool instead of just a piece of equipment for large corporations. The company decided to gear products toward improving the lives of everyday individuals. Apple created computers that were low enough in price for elementary schools across North America to set up whole computer labs in their halls. School and student discounts were at the heart of Apple's business plan from the beginning. According to authors Deborah Harmon and Toni Jones, "The Apple computer was so affordable that it soon became the microcomputer of choice and was found in schools at practically all levels."[9]

This business practice did not just bring in a short-term sales rush. Twenty years later, every member of the generation that grew up with computers in their classrooms for the first time hold fond memories of that little colorful apple that has served as the company logo ever since. The idea that children should have access to computers has created a fierce brand loyalty among younger Apple users. The mere mention of the names "Oregon Trail" or "Number Crunchers" brings warm childhood memories flooding back.

It can even be argued that the attention Apple has continually paid to students of all ages opened the door for them to realize and develop the simple brilliance of the iPod. This method of putting the most vulnerable clients first is a major factor in Apple's ability to remain an independent power player in an industry that sometimes seems to single-handedly keep many mergers-and-acquisitions firms in business. It is a good example of how a Spiritual Transaction can elicit long-term clients in the least likely of places, and the long-term success that follows.

Ironically, while a Spiritual Transaction with its customers kept the company the "apple" of the public's eye, it was a non-spiritual gamble that Apple took in the relationships it had with the competition that kept the company from ascending to the levels one might have once predicted. During the late 1980s and early 1990s, while Microsoft allowed its software to be used by the makers of PC clones, Apple refused to license its software to rival computer manufacturers. Apple would only allow Apple software to run on Apple computers. The proliferation of cheaper and more diverse PCs, all of which ran Microsoft software, put Apple at a serious disadvantage when it came to selling its hardware. Thus, most of the generation that Apple should have appealed to used PCs instead—and the potential of Apple software was cut short because it would not just run on all computers. Now, Apple can run Windows but still keeps its software under lock and key. If Apple had shared its software at any point, it is possible that Apple might have looked more like Microsoft in terms of dominance, influence, and power.

This is the natural course of the modern world. With many developing nations choosing to skip the industrial revolution in favor of the information revolution, the world is being swept into this new Spiritual Age whether it likes it or not. The organizing intelligence transfers from the individual into the space between individuals, as group intellect takes place. Now this is not some bizarre metaphysical claim, it is rather the observation of what happens when a group starts to make decisions through things as simple and accepted as brainstorming. One person comes up with an idea, which is complimented by the ideas or criticisms of another person. These Spiritual Transactions become the organizing factor of the project at hand, which is rather different from the mechanical leader-first mentality of the old economy.

As we move into the concept of Mesh, it becomes easier to understand how Spiritual Environments function—and how this idea applies to all kind of fields. While new organizational meth-ods are reflective of quantum ideas, the Power of Mesh is perhaps best reflective of Einstein's view that matter is composed of energy at its core. The universe itself is a network of energy; therefore, introducing Mesh into our organizational charts brings it closer to the prevalent influences of our time, as well as a most natural form of interaction.

It is critical to appreciate the difference between spirituality and religion in order to fully grasp this book's concepts. It is also vital as one of this book's other themes—strengthening employees against stress. Spiritual Transactions and a better environment do more than increase productivity—they also help to safeguard employ-ees against the more unavoidable sources of stress. While interoffice friction is somewhat of a controllable factor, there are many market forces that are inevitable in business.

Mara Der Hovanesian wrote a 2003 piece for *Business Week* about how companies had already started to learn the power of introducing more Spiritual Environments to their employees. The article cited findings by the National Institutes of Health, the University of Massachusetts, and the Mind/Body Medical Insti-tute at Harvard University that showed that meditation increased brain-wave activity and concentration. It claimed that dozens of large companies—including Apple, Yahoo!, and Google, as well as corporate mainstays like McKinsey, Deutsche Bank, and Hughes Aircraft—were starting to incorporate the practices.

However, stress is the major force these corporations are trying to reduce through these practices. Der Hovanesian wrote that the National Institute for Occupational Safety and Health found that "stress-related ailments cost companies about $200 billion a year in increased absenteeism, tardiness, and the loss of talented workers. Seventy percent to 90 percent of employee hospital visits are linked to stress. And job tension is directly tied to a lack of productivity and loss of competitive edge."[10]

This is yet another situation where helping the individual also helps the company. Not only are people more productive, they are also healthier and more resistant to stress. This in turn creates a more reliable culture of employees who are less sick and more committed; and this increased reliability makes *everybody* more likely to participate in Spiritual Transactions. Not only do people feel more comfortable, but they are more likely to trust the work of the group. This becomes a positive cycle of strengthening the foundation of your Spiritual Transactions, and increases the fluidity of the Mesh.

This view of business is one that could not have been envisioned several decades ago in most corners of the world. The symbol of the computer networks and the entrance of modern physics into the body of common knowledge have led to our ability to start organizing ourselves more efficiently. And to understand the vast difference between our time and decades past, you need only to look at the business literature of the time.

For instance, in 1956 Sylvia and Benjamin Selekman wrote *Power and Morality in Business Society*. The Selekmans undertook an analysis of business culture, much like the analysis undertaken in this book. But 50 years ago, the Selekmans came to the following conclusion:

> [P]resent-day philosophers of history and religion are searching for spiritual and religious reaffirmations which will restore man to the dignity of his human estate. The problem is not as simple as it appears. On the one hand, old questions concerning the justification of production for profit have never been resolved. Thus everywhere, at home and abroad, spokesmen for labor have added to the older shibboleth of human rights versus property rights, the rights of men to secure not only well-paid and regular employment but also the amenities of life-holidays, vacation, and insurance of all sorts, whether provided by business or government or both. On the other hand, our business society seems to face in ever disproportionate measure—perhaps because of our very power in the world—the latter-day universal moral challenge of spiritual and aesthetic values in an industrial age booming with material success.[11]

We are now at the pinnacle of material success. We have a machine that will cook our food for us; information is beamed directly into screens all over our homes; we can contact anyone in the entire world at anytime we wish and for practically no cost. Our clothing is made of the most exotic materials; no entertainment service is too much as long as we are not going out on the town every single night. We can even work from home without interfering much at all with the efficiency of our employer. Perhaps it is only right that as we enter an era of total comfort, we finally realize what it takes to overcome the anxieties that have always held us back.

Of course, not all twentieth-century writers missed the point; there were some prescient voices that predicted all of this even before the first computers arrived. Jerome Davis, for example, gave a speech in 1926—right around the time the first era of globalization was about to completely implode—where he proclaimed that,

> My statement is not that spirituality makes men good, but rather that it makes men strong. There may be many collars that are as good as Arrow collars, many breakfast foods that are as good as Toasted Corn Flakes, several paints that are as good as Sherwin-Williams, and soap which is as pure as Ivory. However, these other collars, breakfast foods, paints, and soaps are not so well known, while the brands I mention are known in every household. Why? The reader can be his own judge, but the facts show that in every one of these instances, the founders of the business were intensely religious men and went about the selling of their products as missionaries, fired with an indescribable zeal.[12]

Davis talked about early Spiritual Transactions taking place in a world that was not used to them. But their power has not subsided with their spread; it has only increased, because the more Spiritual Transactions there are, the more fluid each Mesh becomes. The more fluid the Mesh, the closer you get to higher levels of productivity and happiness, the closer you get to a real return, as shareholders of this human race.

The Bottom Line

1. Spirituality as an asset in business is not a cure-all answer; it is instead a major factor in the recipe required for competing in a fast-paced economy.

(continued)

(*continued*)

2. A network of people has expanded into networks of networks of people. Computers have moved from a network of computers into networks of networks of people. This resulting global Mesh brings an exponential possibility of mass collaboration in this new age, the Spiritual Age, and the positive ramifications in our individual, organizational, corporate, national, and global economy is almost beyond comprehension; it is staggering!

3. Spiritual Transactions and a better environment do more than increase productivity—it also makes employees more resistant to the stress your company cannot avoid. Spiritual practices, including meditation and a myriad of other techniques can stem stress-related ailments that cost companies about $200 billion a year in increased absenteeism, tardiness, and the loss of talented workers.

4

SPIRITUAL ECONOMICS: COMPANY AND COMMUNITY

Surplus wealth is a sacred trust which its possessor is bound to administer in his lifetime for the good of the community.

—Andrew Carnegie

For it is in giving that we receive.

—St. Francis of Assisi

contemporary understanding of the idea of Spiritual Economics first came from Unity minister Eric Butterworth. He believed that a person will receive all that he or she is willing to consciously accept; so in order to receive the most we can, we must center ourselves in spirituality. In addition to the other issues that Spiritual Transactions clarify, Butterworth's concept gives some explanation of the forces that he described. His 1993 book *Spiritual Economics* exposed the idea that an open mind makes us more aware of each day's possibilities. In this way, he very much spoke about opening up our Spiritual Assets.

Robert Solomon wrote something interesting about the place of spirituality in his book, *A Better Way to Think about Business,* which reflects most people's initial reaction to this topic. Solomon writes that "Spirituality embraces all sorts of personal cosmic outlooks. It embraces environmentalism in the large sense (that is, not just saving resources but an appreciation of Nature). It embraces a good deal of aesthetic appreciation (for example, all great music is spiritual). And it embraces a good deal of what still can be called 'the love of humanity.' ... Business, like spirituality ... functions best when it has the most perspective, the larger outlook, vision beyond its immediate procedures and goals."[1]

Indeed, spirituality is about the deeper meanings that lie tucked away in the corners of your world. It is about the eternal questions and about how to come to grips with things as simple as why you sometimes smile. Yet it is also about huge questions, like what the universe is really like and why. Business is similarly about balancing the big questions with the small questions, about handling individual projects while planning out your next decade in the current market trends. Although this is quite easy to grasp without introducing the concept of spirituality, Solomon cites that a narrow business perspective alone is likely to miss important aspects of any business situation—some of which may be critical to your future and that of your company's. This is especially true for companies steeped in old organizational methodologies.

Corporate citizenship is yet another topic that we can shed some light on while looking through the lens of the Mesh, instead of the humanistic models typically used. Best-selling business author and nationally syndicated columnist Harvey Mackay provides a good example of the dialogue currently surrounding this topic. He wrote in a 2008 article that "Businesses that are committed to compassion care about their employees as well as their customers. [Such a] company makes sure that a paycheck isn't the only thing workers take home ... [and] know that their company is a good corporate citizen that is committed to giving back to the communities where they do business."[2]

Mackay is advocating the kind of business environment that is vital to the new world economy; he is describing Spiritual Transactions and their results—a better use of Spiritual Assets. Although we have seen how companies operate within themselves—using

Spiritual Transactions to encourage the use of Spiritual Assets—the company itself is also interacting with *other* companies and the world around it. The spiritual network inside of the company is integrally connected to the wider world.

The first connections that come to mind are basic—the company has a relationship with its partners and its competitors. Previously, I described a Spiritual Transaction as starting with a promise between a company and its employees. Is it really possible for a company to make a similar promise to its partners, let alone its competitors? Most transactions between companies are material, and the relationship between them cannot be as close as relationships within the companies because of physical and geographical constraints. So what would a Spiritual Transaction between companies look like?

"Coopetition"

There is something that binds competitors together even more than the transactions between them—a common ground comprised of the physical and social settings in which these industries compete. Two companies may not be able to truly connect outside of the occasional joint venture, but a constant relationship exists in the transient nature of their common environment. This relationship includes the physical landscape in which a company does its business and the people it touches, such as consumers or the communities within which the business functions.

When a company wants to improve the ability of its employees to access their Spiritual Assets, the company must create an environment that encourages this. But the setting that a business exists within extends beyond the office front door into the neighborhoods where its buildings are located as well as the home surroundings of both employees and customers. Improving these external environments can be as critical to creating Spiritual Transactions as developing the organization's internal environment. This creates more fluid transactions between companies, more efficient trade, and more trusting business relationships—all of which improves your company's bottom line.

This kind of exchange already exists in the concept of Clean Development Mechanisms (CDMs). The Kyoto Protocols among the European Union, Canada, Japan, and many other nations place a cap on the total annual polluting emissions a nation can have. The protocols enforce the exchange by requiring countries to limit annual emissions from individual factories. If the company that owns the factory has emissions that exceed its allotted amount, it either faces steep fines or must purchase certified emission reduction credits (CERs).

A CER can potentially come from foreign competitors that did not use all of their allotted emissions and want to sell their "leftover" credits to countries that have essentially maxed out. Another form of CER, however, comes from CDMs, projects in foreign countries or domestic regions that have the goal of reducing global emissions. The company funds projects ranging from reforestation to developing hydroelectric power plants—all projects with the aim of improving the environment. In exchange for the projected reduction in emissions resulting from the CDM, a certain number of CERs are acquired.

In this process, a company that cannot meet the required emissions standards without sacrificing profits is able to contribute to the overall well-being of the world instead. The effects of CDMs—which are largely done in underdeveloped nations—are wide ranging. CDMs create new jobs as well as a healthier and more efficient environment. Company members who participate in enacting the CDM are energized by this cultural exchange, and the company gains the reputation of being a good corporate citizen. This is a way in which a material problem is solved in a spiritual manner. The CER system is set up so that the cost is approximately the same no matter how it is acquired. But instead of just buying the CERs, the company that elects to pursue a CDM uses a Spiritual Transaction to solve the problem—and reaps many more rewards.

Corporate sponsorship of university programs is another example of how corporate citizenship creates a Spiritual Environment. Corporations that subsidize new engineering buildings or computer laboratories enhance the quality of education for potential future employees. These corporations improve the environment in which they do business and create grounds for smoothing out future business relationships. Although the basic economic function of funding universities is to improve the labor pool, there are many more assets being sown. Increasing brand familiarity, showing future employees right from the start that the company cares enough to improve employees' education, and accessing top talent are just some of the additional rewards.

Similarly, by putting money into public schools or school fundraisers, your company improves the lives of the families of your employees and the employees of the companies that operate in the same neighborhoods. This contribution can in turn lead to higher levels of happiness in employees and decreased employee turnover as families become more content to stay in one place for a long time. Through such actions, you are not only interacting with those within your company, but you are also interacting with your competitors. It is a Spiritual Transaction, in which you are improving the overall environment where business is being done, in order to improve the results of everybody across the board.

If there were a new technology that came out that improved the efficiency of your entire industry across the board, profits for everybody would become more substantial. Improving the industry's social environment does the same thing. There are certain things that require cooperation that an industry can do to improve itself. Businesses will continue to function without the improvements, but the true potential of any industry cannot be met without Spiritual Transactions, such as putting money into neighborhoods, schools, and other environments shared by the employees of all the different companies.

In the long term, these contributions also become important when the inevitable rough spot hits your entire industry. Whether by dint of a new tax law, a change in technology, or economic recession, there are periodic times when it is best for an entire industry to band together in order to make it through—through joint lobbying, forming industry associations to negotiate with labor unions, or another method of cooperation. Corporate citizenship lays the groundwork for these times where a certain amount of trust is needed. It paves the way for more Spiritual Transactions to occur.

Wide Corporate Eyes

There are limits here. Your place of business is the world, but you cannot forget that there are parts of the world far more important than others are to your company. This is why it is vital to extend the idea of the Spiritual Transaction to the extra-corporate level. There is a certain level of trust in the Spiritual Transaction between the employee and the company. In the more transient Spiritual Transactions between companies out there in the world, a similar level of trust would balance your understanding of corporate citizenship's role. If every company in the world is sharing the same place of business, then it is easy to envision a higher level of cooperation when it comes to community involvement and corporate giving. The story of how one billionaire gave away the second largest fortune in history is perhaps the best example of these principles.

Warren Buffett—the most successful investor in history and the founder of the powerful conglomerate Berkshire Hathaway—was not known for philanthropy throughout most of his life. His public donations paled in comparison to many other U.S. billionaires of his stature—so much so that when his wife died in 2004 and left several billion to different sources in her will, some of the more prickly financial sources reacted snidely. *Business Week* wrote that "it may strike some as the supreme paradox that the man who is one of America's greatest misers in life will probably become one of its greatest philanthropists in death. That reality came into focus in July, when Susie, Buffett's wife and philanthropic muse, died." Buffett's wife betrothed almost all of her stake in Berkshire Hathaway to a foundation dedicated to supporting reproductive choice and nuclear arms reduction.[3]

In the same article, *Business Week* wrote something quite the opposite of the other richest family in America: the Gates family.

Bill and Melinda Gates gave a record $3 billion donation to their foundation—three times more money than the total lifetime philanthropic donations of the entire Walton family (founders of Walmart). It was one of the largest donations in history by a living donor.[4]

Then, in 2006, everything changed. The Bill and Melinda Gates Foundation held a shocking media conference covered by almost every news organization in the world that announced:

Warren Buffett, billionaire investor and founder of Berkshire Hathaway, has announced he is donating much of his fortune to charity. Over time, most of Buffett's $44 billion in stock holdings will be given to the Bill and Melinda Gates Foundation. In the form of Berkshire Hathaway shares, Buffett signed papers that give $31 billion of his fortune to fund the Gates Foundation's work in fighting infectious diseases and reforming education. Besides the major gift to the Gates Foundation, Buffett is dividing $6 billion among four other charities started by his family members. Those foundations support environmental causes, abortion rights, helping low-income children and human rights.[5]

The founders of Berkshire Hathaway and Microsoft combined their philanthropic muscles to tackle problems in their common business environment. This is a perfect example of a Spiritual Transaction. In trying to tackle the biggest problems in the world, the formation of joint organizations to distribute wealth is far more effective than the development of thousands of smaller organizations with rival platforms.

There is, of course, a significant difference between individual and corporate giving. Buffett was not giving away Berkshire Hathaway income and Bill Gates was not giving away Microsoft income. However, if several companies are affected by common issues within their shared environment and there are issues within that environment that affect all of them, good communication can ensure that the issue is dealt with most efficiently. Buffett deferred to the Gateses when it came to philanthropy. Instead of giving equally but separately, Buffett recognized the value in the Gates's specialty and saw that the potential good his money could do would increase if he placed it in the Gates Foundation's care.

In economics, it is well known that when two countries develop the same few products, but one country develops a product better than the other and vice versa, there is more product to go around if each country specializes in its best wares. The concept is already a major facet of international trade. For example, Jamaica does not try to make its own wine, and the United States is happy to import Jamaican coffee beans instead of promoting a coffee-growing industry on its own shores outside of Hawaii. Specialization is one of the hallmarks of international free trade and the globalization of the economy, but is only really possible in a trust-inducing environment. Spiritual Transactions between companies encourage this.

God Loves the Corporate Giver

Specialization, though a basic economic concept, has really never been applied to philanthropy before now. The concept of the Spiritual Transaction opens a whole new understanding of what corporate giving means. Spiritual Transactions at the inter-company level or the international level demand a level of specialization, because the world is just too vast for any one company or set of companies to attempt to cover on their own.

This approach to corporate giving results in far more for your company's bottom line, because it greases the axles of future deals and opens up lines of communication between companies that have not existed before—thereby increasing the potential opportunities for cooperative action and deal-making. Like attending a fundraising dinner, such an organization provides networking opportunities you do not usually encounter. It can even start to clean up the general reputation of the corporate world.

There are entire magazines devoted to taking down major corporations and hundreds of thousands of people follow the boycott messages of activist groups. This is not good for business, to say the least. Kowtowing to the demands of such groups, though, is not usually good for business either. This animosity exists, though, because of a disconnect between the values of the consumer and the company. Spiritual Transactions within a business's environment reduces the chances of encountering such a disconnect, or the lack of patience with corporate mistakes that many activists have.

The relationship between corporations and activists provides ample fodder for a conversation about Spiritual Transactions. Perhaps the most famous example of the Spiritual Transaction at work in this situation comes from the old chestnut about Sir Mark Moody-Stuart, Chairman Emeritus of Royal Dutch Shell, and the group of protestors that parked themselves in front of his house. Instead of calling the police, the chairman went out onto the lawn with his wife to actually talk to the activists about why they were there. They served tea. They had a serious exchange about human rights and environmental issues. And that one act did more to repair Shell's global image than perhaps all the millions of dollars it has spent on television ads trying to shape its identity. Moody-Stuart made it a practice to invite protestors and activists to the table, instead of trying to simply ignore them.

As for a specific example of a recent act by a major corporation that fits the bill of a Spiritual Transaction, you can turn to Google. Google—perhaps the first Internet company to reach the now decades-old promise of being a stable, long-term high-value investment—announced in September 2008 that it would award five prizes of $10 million to individual users who had ideas that might change the world.

In an announcement on CNN, one of Google's representatives said that although the company by no means thought it had the answers to cure the world's ills, it did believe the ideas were out there. To celebrate its 10th anniversary, Google decided to hold the contest in order to distribute a small portion of its profits to deserving would-be philanthropists, so that their visions of a better world could come to life. This from Google—a company famous for its home-like atmosphere among its employees and its focus on developing an atmosphere as close to a Mesh or Spiritual Environment as any company ever conceived. It is also a great example of philanthropic specialization.

American Express held a similar online contest in 2008 where the public voted on projects that, according to Erika Chavez, "range[d] from preventing childhood blindness in India to rebuilding a green New Orleans."[6] The top five vote getters split $2.5 million, which would be used to put their plans into action. The company also held a contest in 2007, where the winner was able to receive up to $5 million for his or her project.[7]

Philanthropic specialization is the reason why the International Red Cross is a household name in the houses that contribute the money and the houses that need it. It is an important tool in the movement toward our high-level Spiritual Transactions. It is how you can give more for less; how charitable donations can lessen in monetary value but increase in productive value.

Trading Mistakes, Trading Forgiveness

Think about things at the individual level. You are able to overlook certain transgressions if the overall relationship is sound. A more Machiavellian perspective might see this as a tactic to increase a company's ability to cheat its competitors, but a smarter and long-term company sees Spiritual Transactions within its environment as making up for future mistakes and future accidental transgressions.

Corporate giving is not necessarily important in terms of world development; obviously, in the long term every region can and will succeed in a free market. However, it is a system in which you start to trade something important through your Spiritual Transactions. You begin to trade mistakes, trade forgiveness. And *every* corporation or company will eventually screw up on something.

To be absolutely candid—greed runs through the gray hair of any organization. No one is talking about the perfection of the human spirit, or the ultimate realization that we should all just get along, here in this book. We cannot get rid of the random, greedy corporate climbers. We cannot get rid of the corruptive influence on the good souls of long-term corporate knights who reach their breaking points. Well, maybe we can, but it is not a subject for us today. But it is rare that a company that fails because of a mistake is entirely corrupt. Largely, it is true that there are only a few bad apples in any rotten bunch. It is just that sometimes those rotten apples ... are the head honchos, too.

Regardless, putting corporate net, just a small percentage of it, toward investing in Spiritual Transactions with the world, protects against the probability of future disaster. Any company with a great reputation can afford a scandal or two, however politically incorrect it is to say something like that. This kind of corporate argument for the value of philanthropy is just as valid in the real world as the activist's moral argument for giving to the poor and needy. It is time people realize that philanthropy is not a normative idea. Philanthropy has to do with company performance and our ability to compete in a world where everyone will need to depend on others. Just as an individual would never want to live in an isolationist economy, the individual corporation can never exist entirely independent of its industry, consumer base, or the economy on which it grew.

So what is the proper direction for a corporation to aim its Spiritual Transactions? Just as the internal nature of a company best reflects the Power of Mesh, so must an organization's external Spiritual Transactions. In addition, if such Spiritual Transactions occur in the form of philanthropy taken out of your net return, then they do not have to occur so much in more profitable transactions like negotiation, arbitration, or compensation.

Spiritual Transactions: For the Soul of the Organization

I do think "grease" is the more avarice term for what I am talking about here with Spiritual Transactions and their effects. Spiritual Transactions are not just good for the soul, they are also good for the bottom line. In the modern economy and with the modern consciousness awakening in all people, a company is gravely mistaken to forget the role of corporate citizenship. But why do we call it *citizenship*? What connotations does that bring to our argument?

In a free-market economy, there is a strong argument that being a good citizen consists of looking out for your own interests and allowing others to look out for theirs. Author Richard Coughlin once spoke to the implicit morality of this when he wrote:

> *Individualism has little to say about where preferences come from, including the fundamental values to which humans turn in the attempt to find meaning in their lives. Moreover, in taking preferences for granted, methodological individualism pays little or no heed to what is perhaps the most interesting aspect of morality: the competition among values that is found in all modern, pluralist societies that leads to multiple conceptions of what is moral. Individual freedom to pursue one's own happiness is one such value, to be sure, but so is the right to some minimum share of the material and other benefits of society . . .*
>
> *The very existence of a free market presumes a moral order that encapsulates competition, prohibiting, for example, one business firm from firebombing its competitor's factories or threatening the lives of its employees. Those who would deny the implicit and often taken-for-granted principles that protect private property and the rights of individuals in market economy democracies might take a look at The Godfather or the activities of contemporary Colombian drug cartels for a glimpse of what a system based on unrestrained, amoral competition could look like.*[8]

These ideas are as old as the free market itself. Our economy is steeped in a social contract where we agree as a people to stay within the boundaries of a certain ethical and legal code in exchange for the benefit of a strong society. Adam Smith's invisible hand promises that a free market's social norms will lead to a more robust community as well. Yet the origins of these ideas were developed in a time where the natural organization of man and his world was misunderstood.

There is credit due to Rousseau's social contract and Smith's invisible hand. These two concepts are historical examples of the Spiritual Transaction. They both describe a promise by society's whole given to the individual effort. Both are groundbreaking ideas that can continue to help our society organize itself. Things went wrong, however, when people tried to nail down the exact boundaries of both the social code and the invisible hand.

These mistakes were foreseen by some. To describe one of the flaws of looking at personal interest as relegated only to private

desires and immediate needs, Garrett Hardin wrote in 1968 something that would become the prophesy of its time. Similar to
how the great economist John Maynard Keynes had foreseen
the Great Depression and forewarned of how society might tum-
ble into it, Hardin foresaw the predicaments of our current day
and age. The paper encapsulating his vision was entitled "The
Tragedy of the Commons," (the word "commons" refers to the
mutual communities people in which people choose to live—cities,
towns, etc).

Hardin wrote:

> *Every new enclosure of the commons involves the infringement of somebody's
> personal liberty. Infringements made in the distant past are accepted because
> no contemporary complains of a loss. It is the newly proposed infringements
> that we vigorously oppose; cries of "rights" and "freedom" fill the air. But what
> does "freedom" mean? When men mutually agreed to pass laws against robbing,
> mankind became more free, not less so. Individuals locked into the logic of the
> commons are free only to bring on universal ruin; once they see the necessity of
> mutual coercion, they become free to pursue other goals.*[9]

According to Hardin, the world economy is a lot like the hills
of sheep guarded by shepherds. If the sheep are allowed to breed
unrelentingly and eat as much grass as they wish, eventually the
supply of grass will run out and all the sheep will die. If all the
shepherds but one controlled the numbers of their flock, then eventually the other flock will grow too large and sheep will start to
die again from hunger. But when each shepherd puts controls on
his or her flock, the fields can feed wool-bearing sheep forever and
ever.

In the late 1960s, there was little to support the great vision
this would turn out to be. The oil shocks of the 1970s cured that.
Today each nation is clamoring for more and more oil, and there is
less and less of it. It is the tragedy of the commons once again at
play—eventually there will be not enough oil to go around. Then
our machines that run on oil and need it to survive will start to
die like the sheep of Hardin's 1968 description. Another example

of this comes from the world's rain forests, which provide much of the world's oxygen, but also much of the world's cheap lumber and many third-world employment opportunities. Greedy loggers are much like Hardin's greedy shepherds, just as greedy oilmen have been now for decades.

Not to lean too far into one spiritual tract or another, let us consider Christ's encouragement for us to become shepherds of men. In this context, that advice no longer appears to be just a warm thought—it can even appear to have become a dire warning. Indeed one way of looking at corporate citizenship is to see citizenship as understanding that instead of being a shepherd of product, you are indeed a shepherd of men. People are now a business's most important asset and their spiritual center is the most valuable thing your people can offer you. The Spiritual Transactions that encourage those spiritual centers in a company and shape your corporate image are thus the most important thing you can offer as a member of the economic community.

The tragedy of the commons is an eternal threat to every company, and thus there are only two solutions. You can take the Realist perspective that states that the primary goal of any group of people is to survive by any means necessary, and try to gain as much control as you can over the resource pool. This will still lead to death, though, because there is no way to control the depletion of that resource pool. Or, a second perspective would center business practices on a more contemporary vision that engages companies and individuals in specialized Spiritual Transactions geared to sustaining the environment in which you are doing business.

Spiritual Taxation

Unfortunately, the tragedy of the commons has indeed been proven to exist and you no longer have the choice of ignoring it. The longevity of any company relies on the continued existence of the environment of its business within. Now, there is an argument to be made that there is already one such pooling of your resources—the tax system. Again, though, this is an old organizational philosophy that is greatly inefficient. There is a reason why the mantra "I can spend my money better than the government can" has spread like wildfire. The value of your tax dollar cannot be as high as the value of your philanthropic dollar in a specialized environment, because the government is being run in a Newtonian fashion. The government sees macroeconomics in a mechanistic way, treating the economy as something that responds to inputs that can likely be measured each step of the way. The exchange rate between specialized philanthropic dollars and tax dollars can actually lead to lower taxes and less gross expenditures overall, simply because of the increased efficiency of quantum organization.

There have been times, however, when governments have led the way in terms of Spiritual Transactions—such as occurred with the election of President Franklin D. Roosevelt. Roosevelt came into office after the United States had already dipped steeply into the Great Depression. The great advances of the United States and her economy had been destroyed by a tragedy of the commons in the stock market. Unemployment soared and U.S. industry struggled to keep up. There is no need to go into what the Great Depression meant to the United States in too much depth, for it is a story we all know and remember in significant detail. Whether from the history books or from the tales told to us by our parents and grandparents, the Great Depression is something that cast a long shadow over the United States' understanding of itself.

Roosevelt won the presidency on a pledge of fierce economic creativity. He promised to try new things to try and buck the Depression, and if these solutions did not work he would turn around and try something else. He promised to not be bound by party politics or the difficulty of putting himself on the line. His New Deal coalition was the result of his promise to the United States, and in return he expected the resiliency of the U.S. workforce. Fortunately for Roosevelt, who died in office, he would see his citizens rebound and he was able to make good on his promise.

Roosevelt put himself on the line by realizing that the improvement of the country's infrastructure and citizens' lives was an exchange that the American people would not pass up. This Spiritual Transaction saved the United States from the ravages of economic ruin. Yet most of the world still faces Depression-like conditions every day—from lack of employment, to hunger, to death from curable diseases.

Even Better

Most of the time you look at the world hunger problem as an issue of just getting the bare minimum of food required to all the people of the world. You look at the example of how in parts of Africa there are children who have no other option but to mix dirt from the ground with lard to make barely edible cakes in hopes of retaining some nutrients. Yet Nobel Prize winning economist Amartya Sen and his co-author Jean Drèze wrote of India, for example, in their book *India: Development and Participation* that "as far as food is concerned, the extra demand for food in India will come not only from population growth, but also from the enhancement of the quantity and quality of food consumed per unit of population. It is the cumulative effects that we have to look at."[10]

It is not just that you have to deal with the total lack of food reaching certain communities, but that others are slowly starting to demand a better quality of food, which starts to pull on the food supplies of both developing and developed countries. The food crisis that erupted in 2008 around the world with serious food riots destroyed infrastructure and drew people far away from a state in which they might make a trusting transaction with anybody. The crisis not only killed people worldwide, but it was devastating to the progress of the world economy—something that affects the health of you and your company. Such situations ruin the environment needed for Spiritual Transactions to occur.

The distribution of food across the globe is totally imbalanced. Providing us an example of exactly how, author Carol Off wrote *Bitter Chocolate*, which looked into the cocoa trade. In a 2007 interview with John Bowman of CBC News in Canada, Off related the following findings when Bowman commented that "One of the ironies you expose in your book is that these children don't really know what they're growing and have never seen chocolate in its final form."

Off responded as follows:

That was perhaps the most surprising thing. It's the fact that not just the children, but their parents and their grandparents, who have been cultivating cocoa for generations, have no idea what we do with it. When I asked them, "What are the beans for?" they said, "They're for you. We get them because you people do something with them." I asked, "What do we do with them?" "We have no idea," they said. But I'm not thinking, "Oh, these poor children. They should have chocolate." I'm thinking, "These poor children should have shoes. They should have schools. They need health care." Children in our part of the world just inhale chocolate bars on the way to school, and that cheap and pleasant treat is something that represents two or three days' labor of a child in Africa, who is unable to go to school.[11]

A cold look at this situation reveals that there are two economic mistakes that lie beyond the obvious travesty. The first is that there has to be a more efficient way of producing chocolate, which is something that specialized philanthropic capital going into the cocoa producing regions could temper. Second, this is an obvious market for foreign goods that can never be developed as long as there is a lack of philanthropic capital in the region. In this example, an injection of specialized philanthropic capital could both decrease the expenditures of the company that uses the cocoa and open a potential new market. As the world becomes a smaller place, people will need to make their own new markets rather than assume there will always be new ones out there that they will be able to move into. A series of specialized Spiritual Transactions can create a group dynamic that would create a force to be reckoned with. This is yet another argument for the importance of such specialized Spiritual Transactions.

Yet if such a practice were to come into place, the fragility of such a transaction must be recognized. As an example of how transactions can go drastically wrong, Mike Davis wrote in *Planet of Slums* that,

*In the urban Third World, poor people dread high-profile international
events—conferences, dignitary visits, sporting events, beauty contests, and international festivals—that prompt authorities to launch crusades to clean up the
city: slum-dwellers know that they are the "dirt" or "blight" that their governments prefer the world not to see. During the Nigerian Independence celebration
in 1960, for example, one of the first acts of the new government was to fence
the route from the airport so that Queen's Elizabeth's representative, Princess
Alexandria, would not see Lagos's slums. These days governments are more
likely to improve the view by razing the slums and driving the residents out of
the city.*[12]

The idea of specialized Spiritual Transactions is a microeco-
nomic one. It is not about convincing predatory governments to
change their ways through direct corporate pressure. It is about
starting from the bottom up and injecting new capital into grassroots organizations that benefit the global business markets. You
can become engulfed by the enormity of the state of the world as a
whole, though, so it is often good to remember that there is plenty to
be done to improve the business marketplace here at home in addition to noting your abilities to participate in specialized large-scale
transactions.

The 1 Percent Solution

So, where are we headed with all of this?

My challenge to the economy and its participants is this: Invest
just 1 percent of net profit toward the solution of global human
issues. A flat rate represents a small amount of investor gain, which
translates into an actual profit increase. The return you receive on
such an investment includes a more efficient pooling of resources
that could be used to argue lower taxes as an industry. The return
you receive also includes a more efficient business environment,
which improves your company's ability to function and make even
higher profits.

The infrastructure is already set up for this—a new movement
toward grassroots organizations worldwide has created much better

ways of ensuring that global contributions reach their target. In addition, according to Lynda Adams-Chau:

> Since 1935, the tax laws have allowed deductions for corporate contributions. The current law allows corporations to give up to 10% of their pretax net income to nonprofit organizations. Despite the tax deduction incentive, many corporations give less than 0.5%. The Dayton Hudson Corporation in Minneapolis is a leader in encouraging corporations to give more toward the full percent allowed. E. B. Knauft, executive vice president of the Independent Sector, researched various corporate giving programs. He concluded that the most sophisticated contributions approach involves a target of contributions as a certain percentage of pretax corporate profits, based on the earnings of the past year or an average of the prior three years.[13]

Dayton Hudson Corporation is now known simply as the Target Corporation, and continues to give several percentage points of its profits to good causes. But even if one were able to pursue a major corporation and convince them to increase its gifts to 1 percent, the system is still not set for specialized giving. So the second part of the challenge is for industries to specialize their gifts based on what each industry knows best and the parts of the world or their communities, which present the greatest challenges to the introduction of stronger Spiritual Transactions. Otherwise, this increase in corporate philanthropy will not achieve a high enough return, nor will it represent the full value it could.

As a final point, I return to the work of Dr. Richard Florida. His work indicated that there is statistical proof that cities with a higher level of creative companies or employees have a more robust economy overall. In places where the spiritual currency is highest, so, too, is the actual material reward found in company profit margins. His work represents the material gain to be made from Spiritual Transactions. In the book *Cities and the Creative Class* Dr. Florida writes, "The increasing importance of creativity, innovation, and knowledge in the economy opens up the social space where more eccentric, alternative, or bohemian types of people can be integrated into core economic and social institutions. Capitalism—or, more accurately, new forms of capitalist enterprise (i.e., the R&D lab and the startup company)—are extending their reach in ways that integrate formerly marginalized individuals and social groups into the value creation process."[14]

Dr. Florida proves that what I am saying is accurate on the macroeconomic level in the same way that Michael Ray provides evidence about the importance of Spiritual Transactions in the workplace. The Spiritual Transaction will lead to kind gestures and will lend a helping hand. But the core of the argument for them relates to corporate stability and growth, and "greasing the wheels" of your future material transactions.

The Bottom Line

1. Spiritual Transactions in the workplace are fundamental to good business.

2. The corporate good citizen now transcends local and national interests and includes international and global concerns.

3. Consider "the 1 percent solution" for your organization and directly give 1 percent of your net profits to corporate causes.

5

BUILDING SPIRITUAL ASSETS

Chains of habit are too light to be felt until they are too heavy to be broken.
—Warren Buffett

All that we are is the result of what we have thought. The mind is everything. What we think we become.

—Buddha

In this chapter, I flesh out the idea of the personal Spiritual Transaction as independently as possible from the Spiritual Transactions that you find in other places—in between companies, in between competitors, and so forth. This chapter includes more specific examples about how you personally benefit and provides examples of how to make such a change in your life. As promised earlier, I now take a serious look at what are referred to as thought patterns.

A Balance Sheet of Personal Spiritual Assets

In an interview Ernie Chu gave to *Awareness* magazine, Chu was asked to give examples of Spiritual Assets as he saw them.[1] Chu responded that he believed they were things like "persistence, integrity, high character, ethics, morals, honesty."[2] When pressed about why such

Spiritual Capital is not more common, to reveal what keeps most people from accessing their Spiritual Assets, Chu spoke of a concept he called "counterfeit currency." According to Chu, "What stops most people is what I call 'counterfeit currency.' Counterfeit currency consists of limiting beliefs and destructive behavior. We treat our limiting beliefs as though they were real, even though they are not. Not feeling deserving is an example of counterfeit currency."[3]

Now I do not think that Chu's description of the kinds of things that could be called Spiritual Assets is entirely surprising, or entirely accurate as you see later in this chapter, but his idea of limiting beliefs serves as a good introduction to the next part of our discussion. I now talk about thinking patterns and how they affect us in the workplace.

Cranial Roadways

An excellent example of the power of brain patterns is revealed in the book and film *What the Bleep Do We Know?* The movie suggests that there is scientific evidence that your habits in life create pathways in your brain that reinforce your desire for and return to certain behavior. For example, if you are used to walking a certain way home all the time, then you are always going to feel inclined to go that way and you can even stir up latent anxiety, or a bit of excitement, simply by traveling a different way home.

Let us recall Dr. Dan Baker's work on the different parts of the human brain cited in Chapter 3. The mind is an amazing system of trillions of interconnections between brain cells. Behave in a particular way over and over again and you set reinforced pathways in your brain that force you into a habitual use of this behavior. You react in the same way to the same stimuli each time. For example, let us say that you meet an incredibly shy and withdrawn individual. It is not that such a person never has anything to say, often it is just that every time there is an opportunity to say what is on his or her mind a wave of uncertainty comes over the person. This emotional response comes from the pathways in his or her mind ingrained by years of similar behavior. Even when this person wants to say something, nothing comes out. Yet I am sure that you know that over time there are plenty of people who can overcome this shyness simply by forcing themselves to talk to other people. By changing their behavior, these people break down the mental pathways in their brains that keep them shy and eliminate the habit of being shy.

As an alternate example, many people have a habit of being pessimistic about everything. This is the attitude that leads to what we discussed previously in terms of people who mistakenly refer to themselves as "realists." Take, for example, any sort of problem in your life. You can look at it in two ways. The first possible perspective is to see this problem as an obstacle between you and your goal. The second perspective is to see this problem as a natural part of the path on the way to your goal. Eric Butterworth, the late New York City Unity minister and best-selling author, also once wrote that "Nothing stops the man who desires to achieve. Every obstacle is simply a course to develop his achievement muscle. It's a strengthening of his powers of accomplishment."[4]

To break this down into a simple analogy, if you are hiking a path in the hills there are always two ways of looking at each incline. Some people consider going uphill to be obstacles on their way to that panoramic view or that pristine lake. Other people consider the hill to be a natural part of their journey. Now both people make their way up each incline, but the second person is able to enjoy the things around him or her, too—the trees that line the hill, or homes, or what have you, are something to be enjoyed just as much as the coming vista. This positive attitude is a part of your Spiritual Assets.

But what I would really like to do here is to provide you with some sense of what any such Spiritual Asset actually is and why it helps you in a business environment. It is all well and good to talk about hiking out in the hills or dealing with problems at home, but the end goal awaiting you at work is not often akin to a beautiful view or an evening grilling on the beach.

Perhaps the best example of the concept I am discussing, though, comes from the world of martial arts. Most of you at some point or another have, either in person or by watching television, witnessed a martial artist putting his or her hand or foot through a thick wooden board. Some of you have even tried it yourselves. The secret behind the trick is not strength, however; it is where you aim your move. If you aim your hand or foot at the edge of the wood, hitting the wood itself, there is little chance of your doing anything but seriously damaging yourself. Yet if you aim your chop, kick, or punch through the board—aiming at a point on the other side of the wood—suddenly (with enough practice) the board snaps in half. This is because you lose momentum if you aim at the board, but use the full potential of your momentum if you aim beyond it. In work and in life, you must aim beyond the problem in order to keep up all your potential momentum, and a positive attitude is the key to making this happen.

Consider again the obstacle and your two different ways of looking at it. Pessimism is an attitude that allows the obstacle to become more obvious an influence in your life. You are only looking at the obstacle itself when trying to overcome it. But if you aim past the obstacle, seeing it as just another part of the road, the obstacle is more easily overcome. That is because you are able to focus on all the things surrounding the obstacle, giving you greater context. It also takes less of your emotional energy to surpass the test.[5]

A negative outlook uses more energy than is necessary in *all* parts of life, but most dangerously in business. This kind of sour attitude is opposite to the outlook needed in Spiritual Transactions and, therefore, you are always at a disadvantage. When you come to see the obstacle as simply a part of the inevitable journey, you do not suddenly love the obstacle as much as finishing your task and you do not ignore the ramifications of the obstacle. You just see the obstacle as a small part of the greater whole. Its negative impact is lessened in terms of that small thing's total impact on your day, week, or month.

This relates to mental pathways because the longer you focus on problems and see obstacles out of their context—as giant monoliths that fully absorb your attention—the more support this gives to the neural connections in your brain that trend you toward a negative attitude. This is a natural reaction. The world is easier than you think it is, but your perspective makes you believe that it is harder than it is. The difference between your perspective and reality leads you to see others as having an easier time of it in life. It leads you to always feel more burdened. When others have certain expectations of you based on the reality of the world, the more difficult the world you perceive seems (as a result of the stress you place on yourself). And it makes you believe that those expectations that others have of you are too much to handle. These kinds of things can undoubt-edly lead to a poorer attitude.

Each time you focus negatively on things, your brain solidifies its habitual pathways. Now, because this necessarily detracts from your ability to see things in context or to see what is beyond the obstacle, this negative result becomes more and more the norm for you. Over time you lose your ability to see things contextually, which makes you a more inefficient person. In addition, the things that could make you feel better are gradually pushed further and further out of view.

Negative thinking is a Newtonian/Realist perspective. If you see the world as a great machine, then obstacles become the sole focus of your work. Newtonians believe that the whole will work naturally if you can just keep fixing the parts that are breaking down. But a quantum executive sees problems as a single aspect of the overall system. The executive considers the parts all worthy of attention, and understands that the part must occasionally be replaced with a different system altogether. Optimism is therefore a vital Spiritual Asset, because it leads to more fluid Spiritual Transactions and makes you more aware of problems in their entirety.

Pessimists usually defend their attitudes by claiming that pes-simism leads to greater awareness of the problem at hand; however, the *opposite* is actually true. What leads us to believe this "counterfeit currency," as Chu would put it (something that appears to help but actually does not), is that the pessimism allows an obstacle to take up a greater percentage of our attention as a whole. But most of that attention is not being used for anything but the creation of stress, and would be better used for other tasks.

Stress as a Waste Product

The productive effort to overcome any problem will likely be the same no matter your attitude—positive or negative. Yet with a pos-itive attitude, you contribute no more energy than necessary to the problem, seeing the issue in its grander context. A negative attitude requires you to contribute far more energy than is necessary to the problem. But the rest of this energy does not just disappear into the problem—it goes into the formation of stress.

Although the result of productive attention is moving you further toward your goal, the result of unproductive attention is stress. Stress is the waste product of a negative attitude. This undue stress then results in Spiritual Liabilities like frustration, anxiety, boredom, depression, blame, guilt, hopelessness, and so forth—all things that create yet more stress.

Thus far you have seen that a positive attitude removes a major cause of stress, increases the potential of your productivity by not wasting your attention levels, and gives you access to better context. This is an explanation of how just one of the many Spiritual Assets is so important to you. Given that, let us return to the issue of brain patterns and thinking habits. If you sport a negative attitude yourself, how do you change your mind, so to speak?

Neural Road Building 101

There is something called an "affirmation," which is of great interest to us in our discussion about thinking habits and brain patterns. Out of context, affirmations can appear to be a mystical idea and even irrational. Yet within the context of thought patterns and neurological science, I introduce the idea of affirmations to you as a way of accessing your Spiritual Assets. To change your attitude, you must force your thoughts to take different pathways through the brain—in other words, you must rewire the hard drive. You see, the same thoughts expressed in a negative way strengthen previous pathways through the brain, the ones that draw you to pessimism and lower productivity. Yet if that same subject matter is thought of in a positive way, your thoughts are forced to take a different pathway, a process that stops strengthening old pathways and starts reinforcing new ones.

It takes a great deal of attention to alter your mental pathways on the inside through methods like meditation, and this is not usually time most people have as individuals. Fortunately, there is a quicker and more efficient way to change your perspectives. If you try to transform thinking by concentrating on another topic, you merely fight against your mind's preferences of following the previously forged pathways. Your thoughts keep dipping back into them, like a car's tires keep dipping back into the ground-down ruts on the road when you travel down the street. In evidence of this, consider that no matter how hard you try to think about something in a new way, you always have those doubts that direct you back into your original perspective.

Yet doubt is not the feeling of your brain consciously trying to force you back into your original thinking patterns and away from the construction of new ones. Doubt is the feeling of the general gravity those older pathways have on your brain. It is a nonintelligent function, like the gradient of a hill's pull on water. This obstacle can be difficult, if not impossible, to overcome simply by thinking itself. Therefore, you must find some way to force new thoughts into your head.

In explanation of this method, again imagine yourself driving, maybe during your morning commute. Although our brain can organize itself within itself, it cannot control the external stimuli coming at it each and every day. The brain has no control over whether the sun will set. The brain has no control over what color it is going to see when the traffic light changes. The brain has no control over the next note it is going to hear coming in over the radio. And the pathways of your brain have no ultimate control over what comes out of your mouth and back in through your ears.

Now, your words always follow from your brain's decision to say something, and your brain has the ability to say something that is totally opposite of what your brain is thinking. Your brain does not suddenly make you state something else to qualify it or to voice your doubts. In effect, you are able to say things that represent new pathways without the speech part of your brain slipping back into the old pathways. Anyone who has ever lied knows that.

Another way in which people speak contrary to their beliefs is when someone asks them a question they do not feel like answering, by saying "I don't know" or just not answering the question. This is not a lie per se, but it follows the same conditions of saying something contrary to what people are thinking.

Your brain has memories of past experiences, which you can access, as well as memories of how you are supposed to feel, which you cannot directly access. Part of why you have difficulty changing the way you think just by thinking is that it is unlikely you know how to access the memories that are the foundation of your current attitude or how to go about changing them. You do not likely know why you feel the way you do, because your feelings just happened to you without you consciously and directly inviting them in. Changing how you feel and how you think is like trying to change your heart rate—you can only do it indirectly, by adjusting your breathing rate, not through a direct command to the heart. Thus, changing your heart rate by consciously slowing or speeding up your breathing rate is much like changing your brain patterns by speaking out loud.

If you choose to start up an exercise program tomorrow, you force yourself to breathe more heavily on a regular basis and to pump blood into your muscles at a higher rate. The more you do this, the more altered your heart rate and breathing rate will become overall. You can go from a couch potato to an Iron Man triathlete just through indirectly forcing your heart rate and breathing rate up through running, swimming, or cycling. And as any sprinter in swimming knows, you can improve your heart rate even more by forcing yourself to breathe less as your heart rate goes up—as you hold your breath as long as possible while swimming as fast as possible.

Speaking the Future into the Now

By saying things contrary to your negative attitudes out loud, you force development into new pathways. The first day you start an exercise program, you often feel silly or weak while breaking your old habits. The same is true with affirmations. The practice of saying what is really true, or what you believe to be the best outcome, out loud to yourself, naturally makes you feel ridiculous. If anything, the sound of your own voice contradicting what is going on inside your head simply feels weird. In fact, this anxiety can even keep you from saying those things, period. *Think about that for a second ...* the brain's pathways, about which you had no knowledge, and which you did not consciously create, were settling into your head. These pathways have enough control over you—through how those pathways make you feel when you try to change your mind—to convince you that it would be a bad idea to think more efficiently and become a happier person. It is stunning to think that most of us allow the inefficiency in our brain to rule over us without us even noticing.

That is a frightening statement if I ever heard one. Your brain creates its own prison, holding you back without your knowing it. As so many people have said in the past, you are too often your own worst enemy. There have been many people to expound on the positive benefits of affirmations, perhaps none so famously as Unity founder Charles Fillmore. As an example of how the power of the mind can work to your advantage in a financial sense, Fillmore wrote in his 1936 book *Prosperity* that,

> *If your money supply is low or your purse seems empty, take it in your hands and bless it. See it filled with the living substance ready to become manifest ... Do not take anyone's word for it, but try the law for yourself. The other fellow's realization of substance will not guarantee your supply. You must become conscious of it for yourself. Identify yourself with substance until you make it yours; it will change your finances, destroy your fears, stop your worries ...*[6]

So what are the things you can say to start yourself on the journey to being able to access your most valuable Spiritual Assets? Let us return to the idea of that obstacle at work, as I am sure you have encountered one recently, or not so recently, that comes to mind. Now, instead of just thinking how crappy it was, or how it made you feel—this is the waste product of undue concern and attention—think about something positive that the fixing of this obstacle did or will lead to.

Perhaps this positive outcome will be your ability to resume doing something you like better, or perhaps the outcome will be the praise of your employer. Maybe it is just the good feeling of a job well done or the feeling of a job that is *finally* over. Whatever it is, place that new thought in your head. Now say aloud, "This [insert problem here] will lead to the following positive outcomes ..." Examples of possible problems and paired solutions might include:

- "This delay of potential business is allowing me to become a better account manager."
- "Losing one of my best people has taught me how to hire better teams and to continue to find people that fit into the organization better than their predecessors."
- "A lack of funding is showing me how to prevent this later on down the road and how to secure more funding in the future."

An example of this kind of thought process comes from Jimmy Devellano, general manager (GM) of the Detroit Red Wings NHL franchise during the late 1980s. Under Devellano's watch, according to an interview he gave in September 2009, at least a third of the Red Wings roster was observed to have either serious drinking or drug problems. In 2009, substance abuse problems among professional athletes is a significant cultural touchstone, but in 1989 it was something that most people ignored.

During the summers, while most GMs were concerned about finalizing contract extensions and preparing for the new season—doing what it took to win as many games as possible—Devellano chose to add a second task onto the top of his busy days. Six of his players, out of his squad of 18, were enrolled in Alcoholics Anonymous. And Devellano made it his duty to drive those players to their meetings each and every time, to guarantee they made it. This was not just a simple act of generosity though, for as Devellano said, "I needed that like I needed a hole in the head ... Spending your summer with recovering alcoholics is no picnic when you don't have a drinking problem yourself."[7]

But according to the interview, "Devellano says he did it because he was being paid to win hockey games, and sober and straight players gave him a better chance to achieve that. 'I could pat myself on the back and say I did it because they were great kids and I wanted them to have good lives,' he said. 'Those things are true, but mainly I wanted them to be great hockey players. I'm coming clean here.'"[8] Devellano talked about "coming clean" because there was a business motive and a positive business result that were linked to this act of human kindness. Other GMs were consumed with the everyday business of making the team run. Devellano's Spiritual Transactions opened him up to new possibilities—a sober team was a better team, and there was something he could do about that. After this, much success resulted for both Devellano and Detroit. Devellano is now senior vice president with the Red Wings organization, a team that has been considered the dynasty of its generation for the past 15 years.

Repeating the opposite of what you are thinking and stating the positive aspects of these problems aloud may seem stupid to you at first—that is the feeling of your brain fighting against you. But if every time you think of the obstacle before you, you force yourself to say the best outcomes and best perspective out loud, you will begin to circumvent your old brain patterns. Each time you force yourself to say those things out loud, they will become truer to you, because you create different habitual pathways—the things that make you feel that what you think are true—though it may take a while. It may take several obstacles before you see that the results you talk about aloud are indeed the only consequential outcomes of surpassing each obstacle. The outcome of the obstacle will always be the same. How that outcome is defined is something you can control.

If you define an obstacle as something that is good, then you will spend less time on it and create less stress. If you define an obstacle as something that is bad, all the trappings of negative thoughts dig in their heels. There are other things you can do in terms of affirmations as well. For instance, if you are not looking forward to something in your life, you can affirm something that you are looking forward to in order to not spend undue time paying attention to things you do not want to do. You can, for example, spend the whole day thinking about how much you are not looking forward to cleaning the house. But if the house must be cleaned regardless of how you feel, why would you waste even more of your day than necessary on the idea of it?

If you make positive statements about events and situations that you are inclined to view negatively—and talk out loud about things you like instead of quietly thinking about those you do not like—you can circumvent your harmful thinking patterns. These kinds of statements slowly force your brain to become more positive. You switch away from the reptilian part of your brain and open yourself up more to Spiritual Transactions through accessing your Spiritual Assets. It really is *that* easy. This method can literally turn your life around, because our brains are organized not around facts, but beliefs. It is said that everything you know in your head is basically a true, justified belief—nothing more. Therefore, what people refer to as knowledge is really just a system of organized beliefs.

Centuries of Newtonian paradigms and Newtonian policy is one of the reasons why such negativity exists within the system, as was explained by showing the difference between Newtonian problem solving and quantum problem solving. Whether you call it pessimism, being a realist, or being cynical, this widespread way of thinking is the cousin of the faulty corporate and organizational methodologies of the past. It is amazing that you can literally switch from a more Newtonian brain to a more quantum brain just by saying things out loud that reflect how you want your mind to work. But once you really make the transition, you gain more than just a healthy attitude.

Creativity as a Major Spiritual Asset

One of the other significant Spiritual Assets for us is our creativity. Optimism is largely about being open to the greater context of any situation, but creativity allows us to use that greater context to the ends of productive work. Past books have simply recommended that we go take an art class or that the corporate retreat consist of something creative like skits, in order to introduce a company's staff to creativity. However, this kind of advice is similar to advising people to just change their thoughts through meditation: the process can take too long for people to really commit to it. Any program to increase our creativity must be something an organization can dedicate itself to.

It is not surprising that creating skits or taking up an art form can result in stress, because in terms of developing our creativity, these things demand undue attention. While an already creative person finds little to no stress in creating the skit or practicing the art, someone who has not spent much time developing his or her dramatic or artistic talents will encounter unnecessary byproducts—stress, anxiety, distaste, and so forth. I think it is important to instead develop a way to access our creativity that produces as little stress as possible.

You have already taken the first step in understanding your innate creativity if you have tried your first affirmation. It occurred when you realized that the difference between a negative outlook on a problem and a positive outlook on a problem really was just a difference in how you define the problem. Creativity has a lot to do with finding new ways of defining the world around you, through which better understanding arises. Creativity as a Spiritual Asset in business leads to better innovation, a more fluid method of understanding uncharted territory, and an improvement to the look of your work. Creativity does not necessarily have to lead to the next great invention, as simply putting more thought into your external presentations can increase your profits.

The Virgin Group is a wonderful example of a company that has used creativity to differentiate itself. The company's success in new markets like the airline and mobile phone industry—which are more difficult to enter than Virgin makes it look—is partly due to creative marketing. Virgin's marketing machine consistently figures out how to directly access members of its new target market. Whether it is through a reality television show starring the company founder, throwing a glass of water on Stephen Colbert during a taping of his show, or using the mega-music jamboree Virgin Festival as a major access point to younger consumers, Virgin constantly looks for innovative ways to expand its brand recognition and familiarity with new potential customers.

The Virgin Group had the advantage of starting out as a new business innovation and making its name through innovation. Therefore, like Microsoft, the Virgin Group has learned to embrace the possibility of failure through creativity where more traditional business models fear it. You as an individual are shaped by the practices of your industry. To understand part of what goes against your creativity, you must understand the pressures against creativity that exist in many companies. So how do you access this Spiritual Asset on your own?

Developing Spiritual Assets

A great example of how to do this is the process that we actually used when I was president and CEO of Unity—in which we brought the asset into our business with the following steps:

1. We took time away from other tasks in order to simply meditate on the business at hand, in order to allow new ideas to come into our minds.

2. Once those ideas had emerged, we made a conscious effort to have faith that those new ideas had a purpose.

3. We next spent time using our imagination to try and envision how those ideas could actually work within the current work environment.

4. We strove to understand what was coming to us through this process, and respected wherever it appeared to be coming from.

5. We made a conscious effort to avoid judging ideas while they were still growing and developing.

6. Those ideas that did grow through our conversations about them and testing their waters, were granted appreciation instead of skepticism.

7. We then "released them into the world," by enabling them as new policy.

Let us delve a bit further into each of these steps.

1. **Allow new ideas to emerge.**

The first point is to see that everything in this world can be redefined by anybody in the world. Human society is built on language, but language is something we reinvent all the time. Within the boundaries of language we develop our own contexts and understanding of the world, based in those beliefs that we saw can be changed. So just the understanding that there is more than one way to do things than the way in which we usually do them will take us a long way. Assuming that even the most proven parts of our business methodology are likely flawed and inefficient is absolutely necessary. This is because those potential major flaws are where the greatest potential for improving our company lies. If we make assumptions about our business model, we are automatically sealing off a large part of the potential rewards for our creativity.

Through years of business experience, you can start to see your response to business problems as formulaic. Every formula serves its purpose, but there are often ways in which it can be improved and there are often other formulas that would serve your purpose better—or at least complement your current thinking quite nicely. It is easy to think that you have come this far in life and done okay for yourself up until this point—the old "if it ain't broke, don't fix it" approach. It is true that while you may have some complaints and might want to start working at a higher level, you already have valuable skills and experience. You cannot throw it all out the window.

As a board member of the Association for Global New Thought (AGNT) I am frequently part of what we call a Visioning Process initiated by board member Michael Beckwith, who was famously featured in the best-selling book and film *The Secret*. We spend time in silence to allow new ideas for the organization to percolate and appear. We capture all the words, images, sounds, and feelings that have appeared as each member articulates them in turn. The most amazing part

of this experience is that frequently many different people in
our group will have the same vision, about something that res-
onates with the whole group. This is just one example of how
finding myself the space to envision new ideas has worked for
me in the past.

2. **Have faith in the purpose of ideas.**

The second point in the creativity of business is to believe
in yourself and have faith in your abilities. Self-confidence is
something that can either encourage creativity or diminish it,
depending on how much of it you have. Affirmations are a
great way to begin to build confidence, because they encourage you to state out loud all of the things about yourself that
are excellent and good—which can help to quell self-doubts.
In the same way you learned that you can alter your outlook
on life, you can also counteract any doubt that you might feel
about your own abilities. Affirm out loud to yourself that you
are able and that people see that in you. Contradict anything
in your head that leads you away from the knowledge of your
own self-worth.

Now many advice writers see self-confidence as a point
within itself, but in terms of how this translates into business
and your Spiritual Assets, I must take this several steps further.
While you are certain to reduce your stress level by improving
self-confidence, it is just one ingredient in the all-important
Spiritual Asset of creativity. Many people see self-confidence
as a luxury because it does not seem to lead to any tangible
result; yet increasing this quality establishes a Spiritual Transaction with yourself—something that might not have a clear
reward in the beginning, but inevitably leads to such Spiritual
Assets as those I am currently discussing.

A major part of accessing your Spiritual Assets comes from
Spiritual Transactions that you make within yourself. The affirmation you make to change your attitude does not have a clear
outcome in the beginning, but the effort to change your attitude is essentially a promise you make to yourself in exchange
for self-improvement. Remember that as your brain pathways

have developed you into a person, that does not necessarily reflect what you want for yourself. You are, in a sense, two different people at the same time. Your potential self is making a pledge to your actual self, in an effort to bring the two closer together. The result of this is an even deeper reduction in stress—stress that is a byproduct of your struggle against yourself and the undue attention this draws away from other things. Self-confidence is the result of those two parts of you coming closer together, eliminating self-doubt. You must aim beyond where you think you can go in order to transcend your own limitations.

3. **Use imagination to see how ideas can work.**

Once you are fairly confident in yourself, use your imagination to play with the different ways you are able to see the world. Imagination is simply whatever goes on inside that head of yours while it is thinking about that new idea. Every thought is a part of the imagination. Every image and everything you think might happen during this thought process is a part of it, too. Many people do not understand that they use their imagination all the time. This is especially true for all those realists or pessimists who predict negative outcomes on the horizon when none actually exist. The imagination is something that does not need to be developed, a natural part in all of us that can be used by your creativity or your negativity. Negativity will use the imagination to create all sorts of nonexistent problems or potential issues that never arise but cause you stress. Creativity will use the imagination to create solutions for problems that do exist and patches for any potential problem that might arise, thus reducing stress.

Having an imagination does not mean that you have to be a great artist; it just means that you can play around with how you define your world. The traditional image of imagination lies in the creation of entirely new worlds, but this is just part of the imagination. Thinking about new ways of defining your own world, no matter how small the change, is just as much a part of the imagination as creating worlds unto themselves.

This can be further illuminated within the context of the following example. Your desk at work is either organized or disorganized in a way that is probably typical of yourself. That desk is a part of your world. If you were to reorganize your desk in a way that fits how you work better, that would be redefining your world. If you were to completely reorganize it and see how the way you work changed relative to this new environment, that would be creating a new world unto itself.

There is an ancient Chinese practice called feng shui that gives some sense of what can happen when you shift your world around like this. Writer Monte Enbysk wrote about reorganizing your desk according to feng shui once, stating, "[Are you] [i]nterested in career advancement? 'North' governs career and business success. So you might position your computer terminal at the north end of your desk ... placing certificates of achievement and other awards in the north sector of your office gives an energy boost that could help you meet your business goals."[9]

The idea is not that a new arrangement invokes some kind of earth magic that will hocus pocus your way to a new promotion. These kinds of arrangements simply alter the way you function in your environment. If your accolades are all around your computer screen, then you are more likely to look at them and these positive images become a bigger part of your immediate attention during times of stress. In addition, if you are conscious about how things are arranged in your environment, this creates positive mental pathways that reflect an appreciation of where you are and the fact that you want your life to change. It is an act like an affirmation that turns your idea about being more efficient into a physical reality that even the most doubt-filled thoughts must contend with. Not to mention that if you care more about where you work, you start to care more about the work you do. Feng shui is one example of how simple imagination work can start to improve your environment and make it more ready for creative work.

Another use of your imagination might be to address a co-worker in a different way. Many times you will encounter an impasse when talking to someone else, where two people endure a miscommunication or where both people think they know what is going on but do not know that the other person is thinking something different. One or both people may also be confused. Imaginative work under these auspices could include simply asking the person the same question in a different way. Often this difference will lead the discussion along a path that cures the miscommunication, or at least allows more time for the miscommunication to be sorted out.

There is power in a question. Change the way you ask questions. This change takes a certain amount of confidence, which is why the first two steps of accessing your creativity are important. The imagination is the palette on which you use this creativity.

4. **Divine ideas versus ego impulses.**

The fourth point in accessing your creativity is to understand what comes out of your imagination. You have already moved in this direction, because this step merely means taking the ideas from your imagination and placing them out in the real world. Put them in context with your actual situation to start to build a bridge between the imagination in the mind and the results of the environment outside of you.

Sitting with new ideas for a while gives you a chance to "feel" the context of each idea. Is it truly the hatching of something new that is for the good purpose of others? Or, is it an impulsive, reactive thought that will only serve yourself? This is critical in the long-term development of your ability to allow your creativity to provide you an expression of something of value for many, not just yourself—and the more people an idea serves, the greater an impact it can have.

5. **Avoid judging new ideas.**

Do not prematurely squelch new ideas. Let them fully emerge as creativity starts to arise. Put forward your imaginative suggestions and then adapt them based on results. If your different tone works, try finding a way of adapting it further into your future communications. If it fails, figure out why it failed and apply those lessons to the lessons you learned from your traditional method of doing things. In this way, both successes and failures in imaginative work will always lead to a better conclusion overall. You can find the solution to the problem or find out more about the problem itself, which brings you closer to the eventual conclusion. Edison failed hundreds of times before he created the electric filament that would change the world forever. Instead of saying that he had failed a thousand times, Edison said, "We now know a thousand ways how not to build a light bulb."

6. **Form appreciation for new ideas.**

After the fifth point, it is time to appreciate the results. In order to reinforce the creative pathways you open up in your brain, you must spend time recognizing the positive benefits of the imaginative work and comparing them to what would have happened otherwise. Whether it is thinking with pride about the result or openly discussing your change of tactics with others, this is a critical step.

7. **Release the new idea into the universe.**

This seventh and final point is to continue on with what you are doing, releasing imaginative work into your environment time and time again. Allow the idea to expand and attract others. The more you practice, the better you will get, until it eventually becomes your preferred method of thought and activity. By definition, creativity forces your brain out of its habitual path. Creativity allows you to make better sense of the world around you and to give you a better sense of yourself.

Reverend Ernie Chu lists qualities like persistence, integrity, honesty, and ethics as Spiritual Assets. However, I see these instead as the result of accessing our actual Spiritual Assets like creativity, positive attitude, and openness. Honesty comes from trusting, which is derived from the positive attitude and the openness that repeated Spiritual Transactions develop. Integrity is a reputation earned from being dependable, and that is something that is likely to occur if you engage in Spiritual Transactions.

There are doubtlessly more Spiritual Assets out there; however, my purpose is not to list each and every one of them. I merely want to point you in a direction where you can discover and then access these qualities. What you find within your spiritual toolbox is somewhat of a personal journey of exploration. The goal is to create an explorative and positive attitude prone to creativity and openness. This is the first goal of the individual who is attempting to make Spiritual Transactions a norm for themselves.

The Bottom Line

1. Our collective organizational and global Spiritual Assets begin within ourselves and our individual Spiritual Assets.

2. You can change the way you think from negative to positive.

3. You can increase the Spiritual Asset of creativity by using a simple seven-step process.

6

The Beginnings of Spiritual Leadership

Leadership is practiced not so much in words as in attitude and in actions.
—Harold S. Geneen

When you are thwarted, it is your own attitude that is out of order.
—Meister Eckhart

Your professional environment either helps or hinders your individual efforts to access your Spiritual Assets. As a manager, you can access your own Spiritual Assets as any other individual would. Managers are a bunch of mystical Dilbert-esque creatures—they function much the same as everyone else. But as a manager, how do you create a workplace that takes advantage of these Spiritual Assets?

The Spiritual Environment of your workplace is improved through the same principles that improve an individual's health through exercise or an individual's access to his or her Spiritual Assets at first through affirmation. A Spiritual Environment is developed over time and through the institutionalizing of Spiritual Transactions. Earlier in this book, the idea of creating an environment that encouraged Spiritual Transactions was the first step. The creation of this environment requires quantum leadership—the ability to utilize quantum organizational practices and encourage Spiritual Transactions.

Talk the Walk, Then Walk the Talk

The kind of leadership needed is something I taught once in a course called *Spirit, Science & Business*, in which I said to the class, "Leadership is best thought of as a behavior, not a role."[1] The first way to encourage the Spiritual Assets of your employees is to develop these assets within yourself first. That is easier said than done, and a quick turnaround at your company likely requires you to make the shift into a Spiritual Environment at a faster pace.

Perhaps the best way to begin this discussion is by clarifying what *not* to do. You cannot wring the Spiritual Assets from an individual like water from a sponge. To create your environment, you must follow one major principle: it is about adding to the environment, not subtracting from the environment. A religiously-minded individual might first think to remove things that he or she thinks are contrary to the environment he or she wishes to see. But the creation of a Spiritual Environment is about what everybody thinks, not just the person at the top. The complexity of new economy decisions cannot be dictated from above. The goal is to invite new ideas and behaviors into the environment, not to censor the workspace.

An example of an executive who did this with great success is Chairman Alan Hassenfeld, of Hasbro Inc. When interviewed in 2009 on the subject of fixing a broken system, Hassenfeld said that change "has to come from the common bond that many of us have talked about sharing."[2] He spoke candidly about how to provide the best, most productive work environment possible. In order to help build that bond, Hassenfeld claims that "The first group that you must take care of is the community in which you live, breathe, and work. You must continue to help improve health care and education, because through those, you're actually helping your own people ..."[3] Hassenfeld's comments make it clear that quantum executives have a passion for improving their businesses better, and sees that the best way of doing this is to be open about how they want the totality of each employee's life to be better—not just their performance at work.

One example of what not to do comes from a 2008 attempt by the Los Angeles city council to regulate food industry zoning. The council felt that the people in the poorer areas of L.A. could not regulate their own nutrition well enough and that something had to be done. The council members felt that too much fast food was being consumed and that it was the role of government to force a change. Journalist William Saletan wrote at the time that "Liquor and cigarette sales are already zoned ... Each city makes its own rules, block by block. Proponents of the L.A. ordinance see it as the logical next step ... A few other cities and towns have zoned restaurants for economic, environmental, or aesthetic reasons. But L.A. appears to be the first to do it for health reasons."[4]

Now it is a basic economic law that reducing supply does not mean reducing demand. The theory behind such a zoning regulation would be that over time citizens would begin to find replacement goods to satisfy their demand for food; that people would forget about fast food and start eating more healthy foods. One obvious problem with this was the fact that delivery services could bring in food from outside the region, and that most impoverished people find employment in nonimpoverished neighborhoods still rife with fast food.

However, the very concept of regulating food consumption is also antithetical to the Spiritual Transaction. In order to improve the health of the citizenry, you must get at the root of the problem—a lack of nutritional education and the inability to access other, healthier goods experienced by people in more impoverished urban areas. The idea also misses another point—any meals served at sit-down family restaurants in white-collar neighborhoods have a far higher caloric content than most fast food, yet these restaurants are not the target of potential regulation. In addition, access to grocery stores and fresh foods in impoverished neighborhoods is poor. Bad nutrition is more systemic than the city council makes it out to be, and attempts to solve the problem through indirect prohibition do not follow the true interests of Los Angelenos. By making the people's struggle for food even worse, the problem becomes bigger and distracts them from being able to do other things—time that could be spent on nutritional education and other community fixes.

To affect such neighborhoods it is perhaps best to look to a community-oriented leader like the late Stanley Williams. Williams was a notorious Los Angeles gang leader sentenced to death in 1981 and who ended his life being nominated several times for both the Nobel Peace Prize and Nobel Prize for Literature. These nominations came in response to several books he decided to write in the mid-1990s targeted at high-risk youth. His former stature in the formative years of the Los Angeles area Crips gang allowed him to convince youth all over the United States that the allure of gang life would result in only their ruin. Although he spent most of his life as a terror to society, Williams ended his life exhibiting great gestures of actual leadership.

Williams knew that he did not have the ability to lecture kids into line and away from gang influences. Instead, he shared his experiences and was able to find common ground with at-risk youth. He provided them with knowledge and education, instead of trying to dissuade the youth based purely on the possible evils of gang life. He offered his experience in expectation that this experience would serve as an albatross for inner-city youth. This is an example of leadership through Spiritual Transaction—it was his behavior that influenced people, not his role. It was his ability to open up that made people respect him, not any sort of high-flying rhetoric. Although there is no doubt that morally the city councilors have led much better lives, great leadership often arises from the most unlikely places.

Rose Edmonds, of USA Today, reported in 2002 that "What workers say makes them happy greatly differs from what HR professionals think, [a recent] survey showed. While employees ranked job security and benefits as most important, HR professionals thought employees wanted good communication with management and recognition. HR professionals placed job security and benefits ... as No. 4 and No. 6, respectively."[5]

Will Real Job Security Please Stand Up?

Job security is derived directly from the Spiritual Environment. When all employees feel positively about their workplace and get along with their colleagues, they do not worry about being let go as much. Anxiety about losing one's job significantly hinders productivity. It takes up more attention than it needs to, thereby creating excess stress. This stress should not exist at all because it is the byproduct of a nonproductive activity. Benefits make the employee healthier and diminish undue concern about the possibility of large medical, child care, or other bills that might cast a shadow over their thoughts.

Job security and benefits are integral parts of a Spiritual Environment; they relate directly to how easily a person can access his or her Spiritual Assets. Although some human resource professionals claim that recognition or communication is the most critical aspect, you have already seen where that disconnect comes from. Management communication and recognition are the only ways in which a quantum executive can develop a more Spiritual Environment. They make people more open to sharing their Spiritual Assets with the company and create a place where more Spiritual Transactions can occur. But this is just the means by which you can achieve your result, not the results themselves. If an employee suffers from undue stress and his or her life's needs are not being met, then those Spiritual Assets are locked down and inaccessible. After all, only the individual—not the management—can access them.

Management communication and recognition ought to be seen as more important to the company, not to the employee. These methods create the environment where more profitable business takes place and creates the environment where job security is experienced. The things that employees feel are most important are those that remove focus on their lives and reduce stress levels. This encourages development of the Spiritual Environment, and reflects the common ground the management always has with their employees. Everybody wants lower stress and a more comfortable life; everyone wants the conditions that compose a Spiritual Environment.

Another person who looked into the role of spirituality in business is writer Donald Harrington. Harrington wrote that "Business is a very small part of life, but a part that should enhance and improve the quality of the rest of our lives ... If we confuse the place where work happens with the place where life happens, our decisions will be skewed and often unethical."[6]

Harrington alludes to the fact that you must realize the difference between the spheres of an employee's business sphere and personal sphere. Overlap between the two does not help spiritualize the workplace, because it introduces external factors to the business into interoffice communications. As a manager, integrating the two spheres will likely *not* make people more comfortable—despite your best intentions.

A Spiritual Environment is not analogous to a comfortable environment in the material sense. Rather, it lubricates the discussion of business and allows Spiritual Assets to be used toward the ends of business, not just used in general. As a manager you cannot look at the spiritualization process as trying to help your employees live a better life; it is about improving the workplace. Although your employees may find additional benefits to a spiritual workplace in other parts of their lives, your main goal is to try to draw out and then focus those Spiritual Assets into Spiritual Transactions. You must remember that even though I am using a loaded word like spirituality, I am still talking about the business world.

Consider for a moment the reaction that an atheist might have to this argument based on my use of the word spirituality. Well, what if I replaced every "spiritual" with the word "quantum"? Suddenly all the connotations fall. Remember that in leading the charge for a spiritual workplace, I am not talking about making the workplace more religious or making it conform to any specific religious norms. This is another example of what not to do. You must remember that I use the word "spiritual" because it represents transactions that cannot be immediately quantified and that tap into the psychology of the employee in a way that improves the feelings of everyone involved, along with improving your access to talent.

Separation of Church and Corporation

Bringing religion instead of spirituality into the workplace has the opposite effect. Our philosophies as individuals are often unique unto ourselves. Religious conversations are not well focused because they can bring about opposing points of view about outside subjects. These conversations do not encourage people to find common ground that is useful in the business milieu. Open discussion of religion is only helpful when underlying tensions keep colleagues from trusting one another. Any situation in which a manager forces a specific religious doctrine on the group is a leadership style akin to what Los Angeles tried to do with fast food in poor neighborhoods.

Author Gilbert Fairholm wrote something worth considering in his book, *Capturing the Heart of Leadership: Spirituality and Community in the New American Workplace:*

> To inspire someone, the leader must appeal to them on a different level than mere motive (internal drives). They also must connect at the level of the spirit. Inspiration is more than rational; it is extrarational ... Someone inspires us when they take us outside (beyond) our routine ways of thinking and behaving and leads us to another higher level of interaction and focus.[7]

Inspirational Leadership: Act before You Leap

Taking a cue from Fairholm, I now redefine what I have been calling leadership. It is helpful to think of this kind of leadership—quantum leadership—as equivalent with the word "inspiring." The proper Spiritual Environment does not *lead* people but rather inspires them to enact Spiritual Transactions. From here, the discussion can move on from what not to do to what you *can* do to inspire Spiritual Transactions in your employees.

Always remember to act before you speak. You must state your intentions clearly—something that can only happen if you follow your own code of behavior. Transitioning to a spiritual workplace requires that management engage in a steady pattern of behavior that does not contradict your sensitive, ongoing efforts. Before you attempt such a transition, you must make sure that you know what you are doing and that you want to be doing it.

Therefore, you have to set yourself some ground rules. Before you announce your intentions, start by trying out new ways of communication with your employees:

- Test different ways of making your way through projects, and take note of what happens. Be creative and try to behave in an inviting way. This allows you to get a feel for how your staff reacts to certain things.

- Try to get each member of the staff a little bit better so that you can comfortably identify any potential issues with your transition. Look for:

  ○ Preexisting tension between colleagues, specific concerns that reflect your new vision for the work environment.

  ○ People who already exhibit behavior similar to what you expect.

Once you have spent some time researching the state of interaction within your staff, make sure these findings fit your own demeanor and what you found from practicing new management behavior. This phase does a few things. Your change in behavior will make sure that your intentions to spiritualize the workplace are not coming out of left field. You do not want your idea to appear to be hypocritical. There is no way to eliminate all of this feeling in your staff, but you should work to minimize it. It also eliminates any first missteps by making your first efforts outside of the scope of the new program.

The Stained Glass Window of Change

Transparency is crucial. The next step is, as I said before, to announce your intentions clearly. Let people know that there is going to be a change in the way the company presents itself and how decisions are made. Make your promise loud and clear. List the results you want to see and the kinds of interactions in which you plan to participate. State aloud both the process and the end goal in order to make everything as clear and transparent as possible.

Open the discussion up to employees and ask what they think would help. Formulate a plan together that encourages people to share creatively and makes them feel good about what they do for a living. Make it clear that this is not about the material aspects of the workplace. It is meant to improve the way in which co-workers interact and how they feel before, during, and after those interactions. It is not about water cooler talk, but about how projects are completed by the individual or the group.

Share your reactions about what is said. Write all your notes on a projector or into a word document that is projected onto the wall. If you are open about what you think, others will be encouraged to do the same. Employees feel as if what they say actually counts when they see you write it down. Make sure to accredit each part of the plan to those who suggest it. Call the meeting during actual business hours, not outside of when work is done. Use company time instead of employee time; this *is* about the business, after all. You do not want employees to think of the program as something that will encroach on their personal lives.

Afterward, speak to each employee alone. In the meeting, ask the employee to share anything that is bothering him or her. Make sure that the employee understands that what he or she shares in the room will not be used against him or her—no matter what is said. Should the employee say something inappropriate, you might realize something about this particular person's future at the company. Otherwise, you will be able to foresee any underlying problem that could derail the group as a whole.

In doing this, perhaps it is best to remember a key leadership principle developed by author and inventor Buckminster Fuller. Fuller was convinced that technological and social development required certain gestation rates, and that to interrupt the gestation period would lead to the inevitable death or disfigurement of the project. You will not know immediately how long the gestation rate will be for your new management project, or for the rise of

Spiritual Assets in your employees, so be patient. You will eventually be able to recognize the gestation rate of the change by observing how things develop and then be able to make sure that your implementation of new business projects suited for this new environment happens just at the right time.[8] Fuller's advice was always given with the end goal of doing "more with less," which is just what you are trying to achieve with the release of your employee's Spiritual Assets.

These individual conversations are not about the overall group plan, but about management. You need the best overall perspective in terms of the people you invite to join this new work environment. You can only get this perspective from one-on-one contact. These meetings also give the impression that there is still a role for the manager in the company, which should avoid impeding natural creativity and Spiritual Transactions as they naturally arise. You need to be on the ball with how your employees are reacting to the proposed change, as there may be staff changes at the end of the day after you begin to learn more about how much each person can bring to the table. Remember, though, that you may end up attracting better people even while realizing the limits of others. The program must revolve around improving company business, not just the performance of a specific group or individual.

The ultimate job security comes from knowing and being known for your acumen. It comes from stripping away all pretension and taking a hard look at the performance, talent, and potential of each individual. If you know these things about your staff, and the staff knows how you feel, then there are no surprises—including unexpected layoffs. This kind of individual employee review is different from the kinds of employee review that is common today. This is a review of whether these individuals have a role in the company period. It is a pass/fail. Once you have established the new environment, you will be able to tell who is just not keeping up. You will have more time to nurture employees once the environment is more fluid. There is going to be a steep learning curve in the beginning because there is no set of group habits to fall back on.

I worked for General Electric—a company with a truly great management system—for 10 years. One of its best tools for continuous improvement of the organization was a periodic forced ranking. Managers periodically evaluated and ranked their employees, released the bottom 10 percent, and replaced them with the best people they could find. This practice has helped lead GE to a consistent ranking in the top 10 companies of the Forbes 500 list, and earned them great profits even under tough conditions. Current General Electric CEO Jeffrey Immelt said in 2003 that "Innovation is a social imperative today and never was it more important."[9] Indeed, Immelt's innovation has included as many staff shake-ups and newly created positions as it has financial investments into research and development.

Immelt is an example of a CEO who just "gets it." According to reporter Erick Schonfeld:

> Immelt has concluded that to power his $134 billion goliath forward, his managers must view GE not so much as a collection of huge, multibillion-dollar businesses but as a vast network of entrepreneurial, Silicon Valley-style—or better still, Edison-style–tech startups ... The result, Immelt believes, will be a GE that looks like an entirely different company—more entrepreneurial, more science-based, and generating much more growth from its own internal operations than by simply acquiring other companies.[10]

To govern one of the world's great iconic corporations in the shadow of Jack Welch would be intimidating enough—and I should know, as I was in management at GE while Welch was making the profit-bearing decisions that would eventually lead to him being hired into the top position. To recognize that drastic changes in how the company could be run in the twenty-first century within this shadow is fairly astounding; even more so when you consider that Immelt began this process back in 2003 to 2004, long before the economic crash of 2008. Without his guidance, there is no telling what kind of damage the collapse of the Newtonian economy could have had on General Electric. GE as a financial firm could have completely dissolved like Bear Stearns, or in the much more disturbing fashion of Lehman Brothers. Instead, GE is fast becoming a leader of the corporate world down the rocky path to a new kind of globalized economy.

Forming the Spiritual Environment

So what might be included in a Spiritual Environment? Transparent brainstorming sessions as a group are good for getting people to talk to one another. Another tactic early on is to hire temporary workers to take on any excess work, which would usually get passed onto someone else while these reorganizational tasks are being reviewed. If someone is working at capacity and doing a good job, this should not result in friction among the staff because the excess work provided by the change in how things are being managed has to get done by someone else who may become embittered. That excess work should eventually become absorbed by the group through the increased efficiency of the work group as a whole, though, eliminating the need for these temps. A major concern of any employee is increased workload, and the goal is to increase the productivity of the workload and not the number of hours required to achieve higher standards.

You can also encourage creative input by dividing a specific project among the staff instead of assigning one to each. Specialize/delegate the work to those who seem to do one aspect of the job the best, as each employee is likely to take to different parts of a project with greater success. Also, at the end of the project, a group brainstorming session over the results of the overall project gets people used to criticizing each other's work without fear of rejection. These are just some ideas of how to speed the progress of your Spiritual Transactions.

The overall goal to keep in mind is for the staff itself to develop the plan that works best for them. This often leads to less radical changes than the ones I have described, which usually yield better results. Just getting your employees to start asking questions without feeling badly about themselves, or to get them to share their ideas about improving the business done in their workplace can lead to a significant increase in the spirituality of the workplace. The goal of this process does not have to be sweeping; smaller changes can be just as satisfying in terms of your company's bottom line.

A Corporate Spiritual Retreat

There are other ways to increase the spirituality of your workplace, which can occur when you start thinking outside of the box. One example comes from the Xerox Corporation, which has become quite famous for its use of the "vision quests" that it has a history of sending employees on. Michelle Conlin wrote an article on this example for *Business Week* in November 1999. She reported that Xerox had decided to send 300 employees from all different levels of the company on a vision quest.

According to Conlin:

> *Alone for 24 hours with nothing more than sleeping bags and water jugs in New Mexico's desert or New York's Catskill Mountains, the workers have communed with nature, seeking inspiration and guidance about building Xerox's first digital copier-fax-printer. One epiphany came when a dozen engineers in northern New Mexico saw a lone, fading Xerox paper carton bobbing in a swamp of old motor oil at the bottom of a pit. They vowed to build a machine that would never end up polluting another dump... The eventual result: the design and production of Xerox's hottest seller, the 265DC, a 97%-recyclable machine.*[11]

Soon after this success, several other billion-dollar corporations began to integrate these kinds of spiritual team-building events into their corporate calendar.

The Xerox team may not have actually encountered some spiritual awakening in the form of an inspired hallucination, but the environment did set up the conditions for a Spiritual Environment. The event encouraged people to speak to one another about their ideas and try to make sense of them as a group. It encouraged the participants to shed their official roles and become shepherds of their organization. It was more than just sharing one idea and patting the contributor on the back. The ideas derived from the quest entered the group discussion and led to something incredibly productive.

In addition, the experience no doubt created more Spiritual Transactions like these once everyone was back at work, as the common
experience made people more trusting of one another.

Business as an Exemplary Human Activity

From the business-oriented framework developed in this chapter,
I can begin to discuss more philosophical issues. With the actual
framework, nuts, and bolts, out of the way, I am free to discuss
the general importance of turning to a spiritual workplace. Robert
Solomon wrote that:

> Georg Simmel speculated about the "impersonality" of money at the beginning
> of twentieth-century capitalism. Money is peculiar, Simmel wrote, in that it is
> presented to us, by definition, as free of any attachments, whether sentimental
> or moral. It is simply a "medium of exchange." There is no morality of money.
> In thinking this way, however, we too easily tend to reduce business to an
> unsentimental, amoral activity.
>
> [We] leave out all of those personal attachments and obligations that
> surround and ultimately give meaning to our financial dealings, our work,
> and our communal lives. To dehumanize human activity is to forget that real
> flesh-and-blood human beings, with feelings and families, with real cares and
> concerns, are not only the agents of the activity but its beneficiaries and its
> reason for being. If money means something to us, then it is because we endow
> money and making money with meaning. And where there is meaning, morality
> cannot be far behind.
>
> When we dehumanize talk about business, we should not be surprised
> that we face dehumanizing policies, strategies, and institutions in business.
> In many ways, business is an exemplary human activity, involving as it does
> mutual attention to needs, desires and demands, creative and productive activity,
> face-to-face negotiation, acknowledgment of certain rules of fair play, and the
> importance of trust and keeping one's word.[12]

As Solomon effectively states, business is the most profitable
in the long term when it embraces its role as an exemplary human
activity. The kinds of things he mentions are the types of things
that are involved in the Spiritual Transactions, the most fluid and

profitable kind of transactions. Spiritual Transactions are a response to business that admits not everything can be accurately predicted. Non-Spiritual Transactions are based on the Newtonian idea that nearly everything can be foreseen.

You need to remember above all things that you cannot force someone to expose his or her Spiritual Assets or to use them. In moving forward with a Spiritual Environment, there is no perfect formula. It is about being aware of how things are working on a deeper level, which increases the probability of nipping future problems in the bud and improving productivity. The alternative is not that things work just as well, but that they operate at a lower level. As the world moves swiftly into a more quantum form of organization, remaining unchanged increases your risk of missing important aspects required for sustained company growth.

Work as a Spiritual Experience

The main goal of an individual person is to maximize his or her happiness, but the main goal of a company is to maximize its profits. When you talk about increasing an individual's access to his or her Spiritual Asset, you talk about how to make work a better part of his or her life. When you talk about Spiritual Transactions in terms of the company itself, there is nothing except for business that is truly of interest. To see the true placement of social values within this part of the argument, I turn to Paul Elkins and his book *The Living Economy: A New Economics in the Making*.

In his 1986 book, Elkins wrote that:

> *the purpose of economics is to find out how to increase human welfare. Human welfare is a complex condition, the increase of which involves far more than the mere maximi[z]ation of production and consumption. Welfare has to do with health and human needs, with mental, emotional and spiritual matters, as well as with physical well-being and with social and environmental issues. Thus economics needs to be informed by psychology, sociology and ecology, if it is [to] avoid a narrow, materialistic reductionism that may be counter-productive of welfare as a whole.*[13]

It is no mistake that the nations that take the best care of their citizenry are the most economically sound and successful. It is also no mistake that the most productive employees belong to environments that support them and pay attention to their needs. Your company's future is tied to the future of your employees. The improvement of support and attention is the only way to secure the future existence and success of the company itself. Spiritual Transactions in the workplace are part of that security. People in the leadership positions of any company are charged with the future success of their companies. Therefore, they must also consider the value of accessing the Spiritual Assets of their employees and sustaining an environment that encourages top productivity.

The Bottom Line

1. The Spiritual Environment of your workplace is improved through the same principles that improve an individual's health through exercise or an individual's access to his or her Spiritual Assets at first through affirmation.

2. A Spiritual Environment is not analogous to a comfortable environment in the material sense. It is about lubricating the discussion of business and allowing Spiritual Assets to be used toward the ends of business, not simply *used*.

3. Spiritual Transactions are a response to a business that admits that not everything can be accurately predicted.

7

A SPIRITUAL TOOLKIT
AT WORK

*I believe God is managing affairs and that He doesn't need any advice from me.
With God in charge, I believe everything will work out for the best in the end.
So what is there to worry about?*

—Henry Ford

*Spiritual relationship is far more precious than physical. Physical relationship
divorced from spiritual is body without soul.*

—Mohandas Gandhi

I n quantum business, there is an exponential number of aspects
one could take into consideration while making decisions or
moving ahead with his or her work. So much so that instead
of saying that there is anything one "must" take into consideration, one really has to start asking what things one "could" take
into consideration. Most business literature revolves around lists: a
series of "must dos" in order to succeed, many of which are fairly
interchangeable between books.

I am sure there is one list out there that is undeniably the best,
but my purpose here is to give you something more to take home
with you; something practical rather than something to memorize.
That said, I do want to invoke a certain number of basic ideas that
can help you attain better Spiritual Transactions and increase your
productivity as an employee, manager, or business leader. Though

not immutable by any means, these suggestions represent many of
the timeless spiritual practices that I have learned throughout my
career.

1. The Committee of Relaxation

Famous hedge fund innovator and CNBC financial analyst
Jim Cramer once said in an interview that one of his keys to
success was cutting down on the amount of sleep he got year
after year. Every year he would wake up a half hour earlier,
until he was sleeping only about four or so hours a night. He
believed that the best work got done in the early morning but
that the balance of his life would be thrown off missing his kids
at night or missing out on valuable networking opportunities
in the evening. Therefore, every year, he reduced his sleep in
order to gain that extra advantage on the competition.

As someone with considerable power and financial
advantage, Cramer undoubtedly would have been able to
compensate for many of the disadvantages he faced when he
did not get enough sleep. As someone intellectually involved
in what he did, there is no doubt that Cramer developed a
system to ensure that he did not overlook anything while
functioning at the stifled mental level that comes from developing a sleep debt.

But sleeping less is a high-risk investment. Less sleep
diminishes awareness, reduces the speed at which you will
pick things up, and generally detracts from your physical
appearance in exchange for perhaps a few more, far less constructive hours. Often enough, you will actually reduce your
productivity level so much that you may be working more
hours, but you get less done during the day than you would
have if you had just slept those few additional hours.

In the beginning, it can be difficult to recognize the influence that exhaustion has on you when facing a reduction
in sleep. After years of sleep abuse, it can take months to
come back from a permanent state of exhaustion. The benefits
of sleep are widely known; however, placing this discussion

within the context of the spiritual workplace reveals a lack of sleep as an even higher risk investment than it was in the Newtonian organizations of old.

Sleep disruption affects *attitude*, one of the primary Spiritual Assets. A positive attitude is equivalent to a full awareness of your environment. The higher the level of exhaustion, the lower your state of awareness will be. The strong correlation between awareness and positivity is revealed when you introduce the variable of sleep. The more sleep-deprived you are, the more emotionally distracted you become by frustrations, anxieties, and confusion. It is why you never feel quite right when tired; why you relate tiredness to feeling bad.

A demonstration of the damage sleep debts can do comes from the study of sleep apnea. People with sleep apnea have deep sleep disturbed by breathing troubles due to obstructive throat positioning. Someone with sleep apnea lives his or her life in a way that is parallel to those who choose not to sleep enough and also lose valuable deep sleep. It is estimated that the productivity level of someone sleeping normal hours, but whose sleep is disturbed by sleep apnea, loses 10 percent productivity on his or her day. This costs the U.S. economy $75 billion per year.[1] The sleep/productivity ratio, however, is worse for those people who are sleeping less than their required hours per night regardless of whether they have sleep apnea.

There are situations, such as your newborn child crying in the middle of the night, or other things that you just cannot avoid, where a short-term fix to your lack of deep sleep becomes necessary. A variety of meditation practices has been proven to allow the mind to recharge itself midday. Meeting your nutritional needs by taking vitamins or eating energy-rich food helps your mind function at a higher level. Exercise can make sure you enter deep sleep sooner at night, and make you more energetic during the day by increasing the glycogen levels in your musculature. But there is no solution to chronic under-sleeping other than rest.

Relaxation also goes beyond sleep. Even if you are sleeping enough, the mind can burn out quickly if there is no other stimulation in your life other than sleep. Too many people believe that in order to avoid burn out, you must give yourself time to do "nothing." However, doing "nothing" can often lead to feelings of anxiety when there are so many things on your plate. Of those people who have the time to rest, most do. For those that do not have the luxury of time, there is what is called "active rest."

A great example of this comes from former UFC Champion Randy Couture, who has continued fighting and kept up his peak conditioning well into his forties. Unlike other professional fighters who won championships at a later age, though, Couture's training for the UFC is far more intense. Every day, all day, is committed to either training or promotion when he is gearing up for a fight. In addition to this, Couture must continue to keep up with his several highly successful business ventures. Every once in a while, though, Couture realizes that burnout is creeping in, that his attitude is starting to slip.

So Couture drives to the outskirts of Las Vegas, parks the car, and begins to run. He runs mile after mile under the hot desert sun, up the sides of hills and through the sand, but makes sure to look around as he does. He absorbs the beauty of the desert as he pounds the sand with his feet. This is what Couture calls his "active rest"—something that is still difficult and draining to his body, but liberating to the mind. It gets him out of the gym and out into nature, allowing his mind a change of scenery if not a change of pace.

Just like a hot desert run helps Couture in the ring, your active rest can be productive, too, as long as it gives the mind something new to focus on. Burnout is alleviated by giving the mind the ability to form new pathways and have new experiences. You can do this by listening to some new music while you are sitting at your desk; reading a new book that provides a different perspective on the work you do; taking a business trip to seek out new clients; taking the afternoon to work on your assignments in a different location—on a park bench or in a café somewhere—or simply by rearranging the things on your desk for a few days, creating that "new world" I spoke of earlier during my feng shui example. So if you feel that you have just *had it*, always try some "active rest" first before you decide to take the day off.

2. Join the Solution, Abandon the Problem

Sometimes even when we find a solution to a given problem, we have trouble letting go of the problem itself. Unlike those who follow more spiritual ways of doing business, people traditionally commit a lot of undue energy toward problems. This undue attention and energy creates stress, as I discussed earlier. A side effect of this stress is an undue personal association with the problem, which prevents individuals from moving on from the problem effectively.

As an individual you often encounter things in your life that are difficult to get over, things like a friend slighting us, or a family argument. Business, though, is best practiced when you only involve the necessary amount of attention to a problem. The inability to abandon the problem at the point of solution is most acute in those people who call themselves "perfectionists." Perfectionism is something Ernie Chu would call counterfeit currency. Chu's concept, however, is simply a re-adaptation of several basic and prominent philosophical ideas.

What Chu calls counterfeit currency is referred to simply as false beliefs. As I mentioned earlier, a false belief is something that you have been fooled into believing through your overlooking of whether that belief is really true or accurately justified. Perfectionism is a great example of the false belief. It occurs when you do not know what your final goal looks like, so you end up working for too many hours on minor details of a project, making you far less efficient.

Every project—just like every good story—has a beginning, middle, and an end. The end of any project comes when the results of the project function effectively and meet the basic standards of the project's initial parameters. Most business projects are completed to within 90 percent to 95 percent of their fullest potential. To get to 100 percent usually requires more work and attention than it is worth to the market or the company.

Perfectionism is an example of giving undue amounts of attention to a project or a problem, just as the examples of worry or anxiety are. If you have this much dedication, you would be better instructed to utilize your skills in starting a new project, rather than attaining that extra few percentage points of potential in the project before you. The standards of the company are based on the past history of success for that company. Meeting those standards is an achievement unto itself—you do not always need to exceed them and, in fact, this obsession can often decrease overall your productivity as an individual. The innovation curve is usually set for any particular firm, and unless you are absolutely certain that you can exceed that curve, then you are likely allowing overzealousness to waste your time.

Perfectionism fundamentally detracts from your understanding of a project's context, as you become too focused on just the one problem at hand. This creates stress, which reduces that very talent you are trying to utilize in making the project better. In addition, that stress connects you emotionally to the problem or project, which reduces future productivity. You reduce your ability to make Spiritual Transactions, and negatively influence the project and future projects overall.

Perfectionism is the false belief that also arises because you cannot compare your own work to a concrete example of perfect work, thus you believe that there might still be work to be done. This is also related to a lack of self-confidence, not to mention a lack of understanding of the way companies work. Take Microsoft as an example again. The company's operating systems always enter the market with flaws that need to be fixed with Internet updates. However, if the company spent the time needed to fix every possible problem before the operating system hit the market, many more years would be needed for each product and the company would never be able to keep up to the innovations expected by its marketplace.

Microsoft is the master of finding that balance where the product proves functional enough to be bought by consumers. Once consumers use the product, they report any problems that might have taken Microsoft months, if not years, to find, and Microsoft quickly fixes them with an update. In this way, Microsoft has products on the market as long as possible to maximize its sales of each product, without worrying about whether the product is perfect. This is yet another practice that has kept Microsoft atop the corporate world for so many decades.

Joining the solution and abandoning the problem also means that, in business, you might have long-standing emotional or professional ties to an old way of doing business, which make you hesitate when something better comes along. This is a significant problem when discussing a move from Newtonian business to quantum business. The solution to this problem is simple—let the numbers do the talking. Whatever the numbers tell you will be truer than your gut reaction. And if your gut is actually 100 percent in line with future numbers in every case, well, then you should patent it.

3. **The Power Is in the Question**

There is a reason that "class participation" is a mandatory component of many college courses. Although one theory is that this allows students to demonstrate their understanding of material, perhaps the most important skill this encourages is the capacity to ask questions. The world is filled with people who just do not know how, or are too embarrassed, scared, nervous, anxious, prideful, or even arrogant to ask questions when they do not understand something.

This becomes entirely apparent when introducing the concept of the Spiritual Transaction, which relies heavily on an individual's ability to ask questions. Without a capacity for people to ask each other questions, Spiritual Transactions simply will not occur. Asking a question exhibits two things: a trust that the other person's reaction will be professional, and a willingness on the asker's part to learn quickly instead of just muddling through. It is an efficiency thing. Simply put: You have to learn how to ask questions to get ahead.

Asking questions directly to people in the company or industry also provides you with more than just the reputation of someone who wants to get things right and who is an open person, ready for new things. It provides networking opportunities rarely found elsewhere offers you one-on-one opportunities with others, which can strengthen your presence in the workplace. It is also a key way to access the Spiritual Asset of inquisitiveness or curiosity.

Creativity is defined as the ability to seek out new ideas inside of you, but curiosity is the ability to seek out new ideas *outside* of yourself. The negative reaction to a tough problem is to ignore it; the spiritual reaction is to try to crack it open. Curiosity is the opposite of fear, and fear is the main driver of the reptilian parts of the brain. Curiosity necessarily transfers your thoughts to the more spiritual parts of the brain, leading to greater confidence and use of other Spiritual Assets. Just as speaking out loud can jumpstart your self-confidence, asking questions aloud jumpstarts this critical element of your spiritual core.

4. **Personal Responsibility Is the Hallmark of Leadership**

This point brings up an interesting concept in terms of Spiritual Transactions and the development of a more spiritual workplace. Trust is most easily broken by those who betray it. Every project that is worked on by a group retains the promise that it is the group that will take credit if things go right, and alternatively, the responsibility if things go wrong. Minor failures that do not affect a company overall, or an individual overall, can snowball into major failure if there is no responsibility to act as a regress stopper. As the old chestnut goes, there must be an understanding that the "buck" stops here—with the group overall. "Blame" is another example of a false belief.

Blame is a human construct that goes beyond the frame of fixing a mistake. It puts undue attention on things that can be fixed, and stress is created when everyone who comes close to the problem is also concerned with how to cloak themselves from the possible repercussions of being seen near it. When things need to be revisited, people tend to become more prone to stress, especially as they start to feel that no more attention should have been paid to something. This can reveal the use of undue attention in the first place, creating stress that is inflamed by this return to the issue. It can also reveal undiscovered tensions created that may have derailed the project in the first place.

As a leader, you may have to diffuse these situations by taking on blame yourself. This, however, cannot be done without also following up on the friction revealed by the rise of the blame. Take the blame out of the situation and figure out where the accusation came from. This helps significantly in the creation of more productive Spiritual Transactions.

Taking the tenet of responsibility in a different direction let me lighten things up a little bit by taking an example from the television show South Park. Eric Cartman, the foul-mouthed kid who acts as the rebellious one among the four main elementary school characters, once responded to the subject of hippies by ranting, "Hippies. They're everywhere. They wanna save the earth, but all they do is smoke pot and smell bad."[2] Besides this episode marking the last time that Isaac Hayes recorded dialogue for his character of "Chef," it also represents a comical reflection of another aspect of responsibility.

There are many people who have complaints about how the world works, but few people actually do anything about it. There are activists who would like to see the government change, but instead of going to law school and running for Congress later down the road, many just paint signs and chant.[3] This is not the best way to change things. Taking on the responsibility of leadership is what actual change is about. Until you take the actual path to changing things, you are not part of any solution.

In business you must be sure that if you see a problem, it becomes your responsibility to fix it, but not your obsession. This is part of the Spiritual Transaction system. Responsibility lies in the hands of the person who created the problem, but also in the hands of the person who sees the problem and comes to understand it. The example of activists is especially crucial when returning to the idea that each of us is a shareholder of the human race. As an individual, the example of faulty activism can serve as a strong parallel to many situations you might encounter in the business world.

5. **Define Yourself or Someone Else Will**

One of the important aspects of business—especially within a Spiritual Environment—is being able to categorize your Spiritual Assets. Although older models limit the ways in which you can be defined, newer models do not remove the idea of being defined—they expand on it.

It is vital from a management perspective to update these definitions to ensure their accuracy. As an individual, though, you cannot rely on your superior or your colleagues to be doing all of the work for you. You have to present your full capacity in the business world. Hopefully, in this new economy and through your own hard work, that includes your most valuable Spiritual Assets.

A big mistake in the workplace is to assume that your work will speak for itself. It might, but your reputation is helped more so by your own definition of your work being made clear. In order to define yourself, you must become a part of the spiritual environment if it exists, or exude your Spiritual Assets if it does not. Your Spiritual Assets—openness, optimism, creativity, sociability, curiosity, and so forth—are the best way to define yourself in the workplace or the industry.

An example of someone who defined himself under the most difficult of circumstances, instead of allowing the world to define him, comes from basketball superstar Magic Johnson. Johnson was forced to quit the NBA after he contracted HIV. He revealed his disease to the public in 1991. During this period, HIV and AIDS were highly misunderstood across all demographics. The virus had no cure and a 100 percent fatality rate, as it spread rapidly across the world, infecting millions.

But instead of becoming just another victim of the epidemic, Johnson began a campaign to educate people about AIDS. One of his first acts was to go on television with a 30-minute, live special called the "Nickelodeon Special Edition: A Conversation with Magic." Johnson took questions about AIDS from children, answering them candidly. The special was seen around the world, and marked one of the first times that the truth about AIDS was brought into the living rooms of the world. Acts like these allowed Magic Johnson to write his own story.

After his basketball career, Johnson himself became an example of a quantum executive. He began to concentrate on the lack of services available to people who lived in the inner city. The same problem that the Los Angeles city council would use to try and justify "nutritionally purposed zoning" gave Johnson an idea. One of the reasons why crime was so rampant in many of these neighborhoods was that there was nothing for people to do.

So Magic Johnson struck a deal with Sony to open the Magic Johnson Theatres—movie theaters opened first in

South Central Los Angeles and Harlem, then in other low-income neighborhoods. The result was not only a social blessing to the areas, but also a profitable business move. Johnson's acumen proved so sharp that he even convinced Starbucks CEO Howard Schultz to take on a partner for the first time in history, allowing Johnson to begin to open Starbucks franchises in similar areas. While his Magic Johnson Enterprises gained momentum—the firm was worth $700 million in 2008—so did the neighborhoods that Johnson had sought to rebuild. Soon after Johnson had proven that businesses could exist safely in these areas and turn a profit, many other investors began to open their own shops and restaurants.

Again, Johnson redefined himself, going from being seen as a jock basketball player to becoming a well-regarded businessman. You may think that Johnson's celebrity would have helped him in this, but in reality businesspeople were even more skeptical of working with him than they would have been with other people because of the connotations that followed him from his prior career. Johnson had to work harder than others to prove himself and develop a track record.

Johnson was able to do this through Spiritual Transactions. He is quite clear about his social justice motives that intertwined with his eye for potential profits. As a player, he was known to always approach successful businesspeople in social situations in order to pick their brains, gleaning as much as he could from each introduction. The optimism of how he handled his disease, the curiosity he always showed as a young player, and the much better known attribute of his—the creativity he showed out on the basketball court—are all exhibits of Spiritual Assets at their finest. Magic Johnson is also an example of how these assets can still be cultivated regardless of how bleak things look, how much pressure there is on a person, or how impossible others say things are.

6. Prayer and Meditation

Each of these things is intertwined with the more obvious concepts of goal setting and visualization that most people have already come to understand. Meditation is the closing of one's eyes and the focusing of one's thoughts. So is visualization. Goal setting is putting things down on paper that you want to happen and then attempting them, which is essentially the same thing as prayer. Goal setting and visualization are simply more restricted forms of these two practices.

Spiritual Environments and Spiritual Transactions are about breaking down limitations and improving beyond the productivity capacity of old organizational and economic strategies. There is much to learn from meditation and prayer in a secularized, scientific sense. Meditation as described by scientific study is the process of rewiring the brain to be able to accept bigger and better things. There is no way to see something that does not exist right now or does not follow from experience in our minds, but there is a way to prepare ourselves for the future. This kind of openness to possibility is crucial when attempting Spiritual Transactions.

I remember participating in prayer at the beginning of meetings as chairman of the board for VillageEDOCS, a California supplier of Internet-based software as a service (SAS) capabilities for electronic document creation, management, and distribution. The act immediately brought everybody to the table and cut us away from all that had gone on before we had come into the room. The act also encouraged openness and trust, the Spiritual Assets in people, because the meeting began with common ground. We knew that we all wanted to accomplish the same thing, and that we were all open to good ideas about how to get it done. Though something other than prayer could have been used, that is what worked for us. The company was recently named by Deloitte as one of the 500 fastest growing companies in the U. S. technology sector.

Meditation is related to the imagination. It helps to create the emotional and physical space where the imagination naturally begins to percolate. If you find it difficult to use your imagination, meditation can help. Prayer, on the other hand, can teach you that your long-term goals should usually be set somewhere beyond the scope of what you can imagine for yourselves. Any accurate set of goals should extend beyond your greatest expectations, just as the martial artist must aim his or her hand beyond the board to make it shatter.

Another example of this is Carl Karcher Enterprises, a billion-dollar restaurant company with more than 3,000 franchises in 14 countries. Founder Carl Karcher, along with Ray Kroc, who originated McDonald's, and Harland Sanders of KFC fame, were responsible for the development of the now $185 billion fast-food industry. Karcher also started meetings with a prayer, and handed out coupons and prayer cards (the Prayer of St. Francis) to anyone he met. In the same way that the discount retailers of the 1960s were able to create an entirely new industry out of noticing a basic consumer need, these companies were able to bring fast and cheap food to the masses at a time where meals could take hours to prepare and eat. Karcher used prayer to establish a commonality between himself and his potential clients—something every company needs to do in order to establish relationships with its customers.

7. The Golden Rule

I am sure you have all experienced the truth behind what happens when you treat people as you wish to be treated. It may not always work among strangers, but it surely will with those you know because behavior is a contagious phenomenon. If you want evidence of this, consider any person in your life to whom you have felt close to for a continued period of time—parents, siblings, grandparents, love interests, friends, or close colleagues. Now consider what happened once you had been around them for a certain period of time.

Aspects of their behavior—sayings, physical ticks, or general reactions—of both the individual and the people they spend time around usually begin to homogenize. You find yourself picking up their phrases or even acting the same way. Therefore, when you act toward others as you would have them act toward you—they suddenly *do*. If you want to create a Spiritual Environment—or at least an atmosphere of respect—you must behave outwardly in the same way.

8. **Thoughts in Mind Happen in Kind**

What exists upstairs comes to life out there. If you define yourself as a certain kind of person, you *become* that kind of person. If you believe that something will inevitably happen to you, it often will. There are many metaphysical concepts that have explored this phenomenon, none perhaps more popular than the Law of Attraction. The more secular explanation of this concept is that whatever becomes the focus of the mind becomes the focus of your life. If you are open to changes in your life then you will be more aware of opportunities to change that might come up in the future. Another example of this at work is that if you believe something is true, you will naturally see everything in the world defined by that truth. It is the driver behind the stress that comes from focusing too much attention on a problem, just as when you focus on the context of an issue instead of the issue itself, the solution is what arises, instead of stress.

For an example of this, look no further than our extensive conversation here about the difference between Newtonian and quantum organization. There was a time when the world believed that Isaac Newton would never be eclipsed in terms of determining how we see the physical world. The world then saw all of our corporate structures and business organizations as mechanical, linear operations. Since the arrival of Albert Einstein and the innovators of quantum mechanics, the global economic community and new corporate giants have suddenly moved in a different direction, one that mirrors our understanding of the natural laws of physics. Business, physics, and even metaphysics have started moving along the same pragmatic lines. The rules on which you choose to focus dictate the way you see the world around you.

As an individual, what you believe will also translate into your understanding of the world, which will always tint your view. If, for example, you think your colleague is a bad person, you will always view his or her actions with suspicion. If you think instead that he or she is great, you will see the actions as trustful and good. In addition to putting a vaster image of your long-term ideal in your head, you must also be sure that your image of the present matches the reality of the world around you. This is especially true if you are to achieve any sort of Spiritual Transaction.

9. Giving Before Getting

This is the basis of the Spiritual Transaction. To explain this, however, I will turn to something that my co-writer and I developed while creating the infrastructure for what a Spiritual Transaction might look like. Spiritual business breaks everything down in terms of relationships. Every transaction represents the intentions, goals, and trust of the people who enacted it. The best example of relationships, though, comes from outside of business.

If you are in a romantic relationship, there are many factors that become involved in that union. However, there is one immutable law. If you are not getting what you want, then you are unhappy. If you are unhappy, then you will be less inclined to give enough to make the other person happy. Paradoxically, if you give as much as you can in a relationship environment that encourages relationship health (if not a full-fledged Spiritual Environment), then your actions will result in the other person trying harder.

Similarly, you cannot really expect yourself to partici-pate in Spiritual Transactions in business if you encounter a situation that does not respect your efforts; but such an environment cannot exist *without* your personal effort. There-fore, the important thing in business, as in any relationship, is not to get in order to give, but it is to give first and then gauge the potential of what you will be able to get. This pro-vides the clearest image of the potential that exists in human connections—professional relationships or otherwise.

The goal of traditional management is to use what you think you can get before you decide what to give. There is a basic level at which you treat all newcomers, and where your relationship goes with them from there is based on experi-ence. But this is a defensive way of looking at business that is nowhere near as efficient as its reverse. Without making a Spiritual Transaction, you will only succeed in holding your-self back. You will never really know the full potential of what you could have gotten unless you commit your full capacity.

Spiritual working environments and quantum organiza-tional systems require you to give everything you have in order to determine your returns. Newtonian systems are based only on tangible experiences, where spiritual and quantum organizations test the full capacity of your business and your-self. It is odd, given this explanation, that people have not done this more often in the past. Spiritual Transactions should be tempered with an analysis of material results, after—not before—the fact, when things are proven, not when they are merely a hypothesis.

Spiritual Transactions are made in expectation of some-thing that improves your life—sometimes something that is quantifiable, sometimes not. You must protect the Spiritual Transaction against waste, as waste creates stress and stress destroys the Spiritual Transaction. The Spiritual Transaction becomes both the best way to do business, and a gauge for how well business is being done.

The Bottom Line

1. There are many different spiritual practices aimed at enhancing the best business results in the new quantum corporate environment.

2. There are several spiritual truths active in our lives and at work; however, there is no one way to approach the creation of a Spiritual Environment.

3. Accept the fact that there are no accidents in the universe. This will allow you to always look for the possibilities that come from any situation.

8

BUILDING SPIRITUAL TRANSACTIONS

What we want to be is something completely new. There is no physical analog for what Amazon.com is becoming.

—Jeff Bezos

When an idea reaches critical mass there is no stopping the shift its presence will induce.

—Marianne Williamson

hile examples of the more spiritualized companies of the world abound, examples of what has happened to old-world Newtonian companies in the coming quantum era are also present all around us. Perhaps the most substantial example of a non-Spiritual Transaction today is the reason why so many of these companies have crashed and burned—the subprime mortgage transactions.

These mortgages were called "subprime" because their interest rates were below the prime for the mortgage's first two years. But after the second anniversary of home ownership came about, the interest rate would increase significantly—often doubling or even tripling. The idea was that within that two-year period, people would make more money and then be in a better position to pay the higher interest when the rate went up. And even if people could not pay, the value of homes in the United States was increasing so quickly that reselling their home at a profit was considered to be a surefire escape for the owner.

The problem is that most people did not fully understand the terms, and in many cases, did not even qualify for the mortgage. Hundreds of thousands of people bought houses they could not afford. Some could not afford to own a home at all. Others bought houses over the future price range. But the banks and mortgage firms were relying on government subsidies and the robust U.S. economy to propel these home owners into a position where they could meet their payments.

These companies were trying to trick Americans into houses that were just at or beyond the limit of their price ranges. On the surface it appeared that the deals would increase U.S. home ownership, but Americans were instead in a squeeze play that ended up inflating home prices. These prices pushed the whole system too far, so that new home owners were buying homes much further outside of their price range just to get the same product that those who came before them had received.

These companies were so focused on increasing short-term profits that they created a tragedy of the commons event, causing the whole system to implode. House prices deflated to below common-sense market prices; people were stuck with "underwater" mortgages that they could not pay; and the companies that put this scheme into motion began to fail. The mortgage investments were so entwined in the rest of the financial system that other firms began to fail as well.

Yet, if these companies had not failed—and Americans had been able to keep up with their payments—other companies would have gone under anyway. The money would have come out of the budgets for things like movies, restaurants, clothing, vacations; the economy's balance was effectively thrown off. Banks issued second mortgages—which would allow people to spend at the same rate they would have without the expensive mortgage, with the assumption that they could handle the debt in 20 years—which concealed the situation over a longer term. However, this was just another non-Spiritual Transaction at work, and it, too, only made the problem worse.

Yes, Yes, and Yes

There is an old gibe in the business world that refers to the lapdog reputation many executive advisors acquire through trying to stand behind their employers. They are often referred to as the "yes-men." The yes-man is seen as somebody who does not share his own opinions with his colleagues and works only to set his superior's plans into motion. Often this individual is also seen as not really doing anything, as idle or even lazy.

There is also another kind of person who always says yes. Take the example of "improv," the dramatic art seen on television shows like *Whose Line Is It Anyway?* and occasionally on *Saturday Night Live*. The first lesson when you learn improv is to always say yes to everything the person is doing or asking on stage with you. If you respond with a contrary idea or just say no, the fluency of the improvisation comes to a stop. At that point, the two actors are left on stage trying to restart the scene or regain momentum, and have usually already lost the audience.

The mantra of the improviser is "always say yes." Yet this kind of saying yes does not refer to simply following the lead without contributing anything. The actor who says yes is following the lead of the first actor, but they are also adapting the suggestions of the leader and even eventually taking over the lead themselves. Dramatic improvisation is a common tool at corporate retreats and for companies to teach new management creative skills; however, in the context of the Spiritual Transaction, even more value comes out of the practice.

The Spiritual Transaction is not about patting each other on the back and recognizing one another's work. The Spiritual Transaction is about accepting whatever comes from your colleagues and then adding your own constructive adaptation if needed. It is about always saying yes to *ideas*. The improvisation group cannot move forward without the support of the whole, and the way it functions allows the group to constantly move through new and uncharted territory.

The improvisation group has general outlines of things that have worked in the past, or ways to respond to different suggestions, but this loose skeleton is often left behind and at the most serves as a fallback position. Similarly, a company that enters new territory or markets—as it does almost every day—requires quick thinking and total collaboration. What is going on during the improvisational performance is akin to the Spiritual Transaction, only the business environment does not close its doors and start talking about something new every few minutes. Good business indeed looks like long-term improvisation, based in the fluid collaboration of those who work with the company.

But the modern yes-man says yes to more than the collaboration of his colleagues. It is also about the businessperson who sees everything that comes his or her way as an opportunity worth taking. In explanation of this, let me return to something I discussed in our evaluation of the importance of sleep. Sleeping less, you might remember, was considered to be a "high-risk investment."

Moving from the false certainty of Newtonian business into quantum business reveals every move to be a calculation of probabilities instead of absolute variables. Therefore, every move in life can be said to carry a certain amount of risk. Everything that comes your way in life has, by definition, some sort of risk attached to it. It is one thing to say that you must simply look past it and not focus too much on it, but how is this risk properly balanced so as to reduce your levels of stress? Well, by using your imagination you start to understand that stress is often created because of how you define your world. You can look at everything that comes your way as a liability. You can also look at everything that comes your way as an investment.

All investments in the financial world are understood to carry with it a certain amount of risk, as are all investments in life. Every time you have a conversation with a colleague or complete some of your work, you are making an investment of your time. Time is another one of those deeply hidden Spiritual Assets. The time you have during the day is something you can choose to spend productively or to not spend productively. Your sense of how to use your time can be clouded in the same way that creativity or your attitude can be clouded. As evidence of this, think back to any time you have felt overly tired or overly stressed. It often seems like time goes more quickly for us or more slowly for us; you can even lose track of what day it is. This is obviously something that seriously detracts from our ability to use our time wisely.

Time after Time

Time is yet another thing that the world truly discovered when moving from Newtonian ideas to a quantum business world. Albert Einstein discovered that time is actually the fourth dimension that each of us exists within physically, whereas Newton saw time as something that could not be affected. Through the idea of Relativity, people learned that the time dimension is something that can be altered, just as you might be able to shrink your waistline or how you grew taller as a child. Your physical means to control time may appear limited, but your attitude toward time and the use of it show just how much control you have within your own dimension.

Therefore, every situation you come across in life is an *investment of your time*. You can choose to access your time in a spiritual way that enhances your ability to use it, or you can choose not to. The risk going into any transaction, spiritual or otherwise, always includes your Spiritual Assets—time, attitude, and so forth. Spiritual Transactions encourage these Spiritual Assets in order to create better investments for you. A non-Spiritual Transaction increases the risk of investing these assets, which makes it less likely that they will be utilized.

Let us wrap this back around to the example of the improvisation group. Every move made by the actors on stage is an investment of limited time, because they only have a few minutes per scene on stage. In comparison to this, you as an individual have almost infinite time to spend. Keep in mind the idea that all time spent is an investment. Now think about what would happen if you had as much money as you had time. History has proven that great fortunes typically corrupt the spending habits and investment acumen of the beholders. These wealthy people lose their sense of risk and end up wasting a lot of that money. When on stage, you see the risk to your time more clearly and can isolate the best way of using that time. Back in real life, you lose your sense of risk, and your sense of how to use that precious time in a way that benefits you most is lost—because you are alternatively rich in the time that is scarcer for the stage actors.

What I am getting at is that the modern yes-man does not just say yes to his colleagues, he also says yes to the universe around him. He says yes to everything that comes his way, because it is always the best way of using his time and the best way to keep his spirits up. But what exactly does this saying yes mean? Does it mean that the yes-man has to accept every offer, or conversation, or red tag special?

Think of the concept as an individual rather than a consumer. A consumer "consumes," and a consumer cannot always say yes to everything offered. An individual "invests." Saying yes means accepting all the data presented to you and trying to find the best possible way forward. It is where the Spiritual Assets of time, creativity, and attitude integrate. Attitude gives you the understanding of everything involved, creativity leads to the best way forward, and then time is what you have to invest, allowing you to move forward.

Acceptance as Your Ally

Saying yes is probably best defined as *acceptance*, a word with a variety of connotations. It can mean to receive something, to appreciate it while it is there, or to disconnect yourself from it when the experience passes. Acceptance can be seen here as the culmination of several different Spiritual Assets, and a study of it reveals the integrated nature of those assets. Spiritual Assets are not separate gifts that sit in mutual exclusivity near the back of your mind. They are symbiotic in nature.

My own personal experience reinforces this idea. While I was working with an investment group for technology start-up companies called Angel Strategies, we reviewed hundreds of investment opportunities. We chose to say yes to every one of the myriad of business plans we received in a spirit of opening ourselves to the universe for any and all possible investment opportunities. Even those businesses that we had significant resistance to at the outset received our best observation and analysis. While we said "no, but thank you" to more than 95 percent of these opportunities, we were able to see the gifts buried in many of them. In a couple of instances our best investments were in companies that we had thought would be the worst ones during our initial assessment.

Acceptance is one way that Spiritual Assets can combine together to create something that helps us with Spiritual Transactions. Acceptance in a Spiritual Transaction defines the action taken on the receiving end of a Spiritual Transaction. Other combinations, just as other types of Spiritual Assets, also exist. For example, when an individual invests his or her time into curiosity, asking questions of his or her colleagues with the intent of better understanding either that colleague or the point, you see another combination. You again witness "acceptance" when the answer is returned to you. This is a simplistic example of how the Spiritual Transaction utilizes combinations of our Spiritual Assets in succession of one another. If you remove any particular one of your Spiritual Assets from the equation, this series of combinations cannot take place.

Spiritual Transactions can be seen as akin to compound interest—over time the value of the Spiritual Environment increases at an accelerating rate. This is an important factor to understand about the Spiritual Transaction if it is to be properly used. A definition of the mechanics of the Spiritual Transaction shows that it is not just some mysterious occurrence that appears under the right conditions. It is something that can be understood today and arises if the right components are placed into the same place, like thunder and lightning or that invention humankind found prior to even spirituality itself—fire.

Risk as Investment

Returning to our discussion of risk, the "acceptance" part of the Spiritual Transaction is not just an acceptance of the other person. When you start to accept the risk and stop focusing on it, you are able to take into consideration the full reality of your situation and make much better decisions. You can literally reduce the risk of any investment simply by changing how you look at the risk. This is where you finally break free from the Newtonian vision of the world around you, which revolves around focusing undue attention on the inherent risk of the world, creating the stress that disrupts all spiritual activity.

Again—this does not mean that you are *ignoring* the risk. You are instead accepting the risk for what it is, no longer fighting against it, and investing your time more intelligently. You evaluate the risk more efficiently. If the risk is lower, you will not spend too much time on it, though you will still understand its role in your environment. If the risk is high, then the attention paid to it will be balanced, but still draw your attention away from other things. This increased focusing of your attention isolates the risk by making sure this risk does not spread to other things because you have too thin a concentration on its ramifications. You might worry that accepting the risk means overlooking the risk, whereas the contrary is true. If you spend too much time focusing on risk, then you can never have an accurate evaluation of it. Big risks can appear to be smaller and small risks can appear to be bigger than they are because you do not have the scope to understand these things in context.

A good example of how most people react to risk comes from Bill Tancer, who was able to determine the top 10 fears of the Internet-using public—a huge sample of millions of searches representing the clearest sampling ever created on the subject. Tancer wrote, "the top ten search terms from queries containing 'fear of': 1. Flying; 2. Heights; 3. Clowns (which may also refer to the movie *Fear of Clowns*); 4. Intimacy; 5. Death; 6. Rejection; 7. People; 8. Snakes; 9. Success; 10. Driving."[1]

Tancer noted that four of these top 10 fears were social fears. A fear of intimacy, a fear of rejection, a fear of people, and a fear of success are all related to non-Spiritual Transactions and individuals who have had difficulty accessing their Spiritual Assets. Interesting enough, clowns are themselves a social device, developed as a foil for social commentary, and both flying and driving are essentially social activities, involving large groups of strangers who take on the joint risk of traveling at inhuman speeds in close proximity to one another.

I would argue that seven of the top 10 fears have to do with trust—a trust broken by decades of existing within a heartless and incorrectly built Newtonian system that encourages people to isolate themselves into their individual parts of the machine. The four social fears that Tancer pointed out are all directly related to the Spiritual Transaction, which strives for an intimate environment between people that eliminates rejection in order to increase success. Tancer's research emphasizes the need for Spiritual Transactions by putting this information into the context of the Internet-using public, who are considered to be the brightest, most inquisitive group of people to ever arise. The Spiritual Transaction removes the risk of those four social fears, lowering the stress level caused by each—something that could have an immeasurable impact on society.

Morality and the Spiritual Transaction

You now know what a Spiritual Transaction is; now I must define what a Spiritual Transaction is *not*. There are immediate connotations to this phrase that come from old school, Newtonian organizational principles. So in order to really move forward with everyone in tow, I should go over these connotations and dispel any misunderstandings.

The first and perhaps the most glaring connotation is the assumption that we must also mean a "moral" transaction when discussing a Spiritual Transaction. Morality is a tricky concept that introduces normative values into our world of business. Where the Spiritual Transaction is a function of the economy, morality is a value judgment made about the economy, and the two concepts are different. A book called *Emerging Global Business Ethics* described the morality of business as follows:

> Each time we note that people will tend to act morally more readily under certain conditions rather than others we recognize the importance of the conditions for moral behavior. When the lights go out in a large city, when a dark anonymity surrounds each person ... morality may suffer. We should not be surprised. Plato related a similar story to us thousands of years ago in the case of Gyge's ring. Similarly, the Ik, a primitive African tribe, is an example of a people

placed under conditions which rendered morality extremely difficult. Finally, we recognize the importance of the moral conditions within which institutions, such as corporations and the state, may act when we note, among other things, the special powers they have, the temptations to which they may be subjected, and the competitive pressures under which politicians and transnational corporations operate. In short, both individuals and institutions are affected by the moral conditions which surround them.[2]

Morality based on this description can therefore be considered both an individual effort and a reality of the business environment. It does not represent the totality of one's Spiritual Assets, but *a system of organizing cost*. Something that is moral is something that does not represent socially unacceptable cost, and something that is amoral does not take cost into consideration in terms of society—regardless of whether the cost is moral or immoral. Immoral actions bring costs that society does not accept as normal—and marginal social cost as a concept has been known to economists for a long time.

This is something that is Newtonian in nature. Newton's understanding of the world led us to believe that the world should be seen in black and white, and that firm divisions could be found when people began to categorize things. Yet there are things that were considered moral 500 years ago—like slavery—that are suddenly immoral today. Morality changes over time and can never be absolutely defined; however, morality is supposed to do just the opposite—introduce an absolute definition of right and wrong.

It is no wonder, then, that there has never really been a successful effort to introduce morality into the business world. Because morals treat the world as static, they are the first thing to give way when that world radically changes. Dr. J.D. Glover wrote in his 1954 book *The Attack on Big Business* that morality in terms of business must be defined differently than when it is applied to the individual. He wrote that, "In the inverted morality of corporations—as laid down for them by the law—any act in which there enters a thought of charity or philanthropy, or any imponderable feelings of business responsibility and obligation, is not the kind of thing corporations can be expected ordinarily to do. The reason, of course, is that the corporation is conceived to be single-purposed and irresponsible. The norm of corporate behavior is what such an entity as this might do – not what a normal group of people might do."[3]

Judging corporations by the standards of man is bound to create a significant disconnect in the understanding of how to bring these companies and their communities into greater harmony. This false belief that morality is absolute or rigidly defined has created the stress and distrust that the work in this book would predict—which has left a visible mark on human history.

As an example, David Frisby and George Simmel wrote in their book *The Philosophy of Money* that:

> Just as so often the mistaken prejudices promote their justification, so the descendants of the trading aristocracy of that period indulged in a ruthless misuse of their power, whose form and extent was possible only because of the novelty of monetary capital and the freshness of its impact on relationships that were differently organized. Thus it was that the masses—from the Middle Ages right up to the nineteenth century—thought that there was something wrong with the origin of great fortunes and that their owners were rather sinister personalities. Tales of horror spread about the origin of the Grimaldi, the Medici and the Rothschild fortunes, not only in the sense of moral duplicity but in a superstitious way as if a demonic spirit was at work.[4]

Society's dubious value system created both an environment in which financial corruption could blossom, as well as a total misunderstanding of what was at work in these corrupt organizations. Morality clouded the judgment of people who could not properly understand how to regulate the corruption or properly address its results. So where distrust may have been warranted at times, the origin of that distrust was never properly isolated and thus nothing could be done about the actual corruption. Morality in these cases has proven itself quite impotent, and often a cause of pain rather than a cure.

A Spiritual Transaction is also *not* something that damages the Spiritual Environment inside of your group by taking unnecessary risks. I once had an experience, while working as a consultant to Electronic Associates Inc. (EAI), during the development of an exciting new analog plotting system. The product could draw perfectly smooth curves quickly and had a broad market. EAI asked me to meet with a large, possible partner company from halfway around the world. The meeting was constructed so that I could explain the capabilities of the new product.

But the representative from the other country was less interested in what the product could do, and far more interested in how it worked—he even eventually asked for a copy of the proprietary software that drove the system. This was software that I myself had developed and, knowing the value of the program, it became clear that he may have been interested in copying the product instead of remarketing it. With that I had to back away from the meeting, inform my client that I just was not comfortable with moving forward (without tipping my hand), and we easily agreed to end the meetings with the other company. I saw that it was clear that there was no Spiritual Transaction possible because of the intentions of the other party, and as a leader it was my duty to preserve the Spiritual Environment on my end by making a tough decision.

Differentiation, Separation, and New Integration

Differentiating the Spiritual Transaction from morality is as important as separating it from religion. Although morality and religion might help an individual find a better emotional space, neither is congruent with the concepts laid down in this book. Morality does not fit into the Spiritual Transaction model because it demands that we judge our colleagues instead of interpreting and building off them. Every interaction in a quantum model requires the very creativity and flexibility that morality blocks. Spiritual workplaces are meant to remove the hesitancy that people have in working together at their maximum capacity, and morality is by definition the *introduction* of just such hesitancy.

As discussed earlier, a better way to evaluate things in a Spiritual Environment comes from risk assessment rather than the unstable "absolutist" values represented by morality. A better standard to set for corporations is how well they integrate into the global Spiritual Economy, rather than whether they have made mistakes in the past. And although this form of evaluation has already arrived, those reacting to it may not fully understand what is going on. The most significant example of this occurred at the time of the 1999 World Trade Organization summit in Seattle, Washington. In their book *Insurrection: Citizen Challenge to Corporate Power*, authors Kevin Danaher and Jason Mark described the following scenario:

> As (President) Clinton spoke to the trade ministers, reporters across Seattle scrambled to make sense of the protests. The nation hadn't seen anything like the Seattle conflict since the height of the Vietnam War, and newspapers and television networks were anxious to explain the activists' passion to a startled public. The corporate accountability movement, which had simmered just beneath the surface of politics throughout the 1990s, had in the space of less than a week boiled up to the surface of the popular consciousness.
>
> Many pundits expressed shock that resistance to the WTO was so deep and that the passions of the protesters had gone so far. Influential New York Times columnist Thomas Friedman ... said the protesters' criticisms and demands were inconsistent: While the activists decried the power of a secretive global government, they wanted new rules that could only be enacted by such a government. Friedman was right, but not in the way he thought. The activists weren't anti-globalist, they were anti-corporate. Among protesters there wasn't a question of whether the new global economy should have rules. The heat in the streets was over who should be writing the rules: corporations, or citizens. News commentators had difficulty understanding the protesters because they failed to recognize that the conflict was over governance, not globalization.[5]

The protestors were addressing issues that had to do with the Spiritual Transaction. They were against the lack of transparency in the decision-making bodies that affected them directly. They protested the lack of community investment and the perception that the global business environment was not a shared one. They did not protest the morality of what these corporations were going to do, but instead what they were planning to do in moving forward. These issues of Spiritual Transactions were not likely understood by the protesting masses as they faced the gas canisters and attack dogs of the local authorities, but it is an example of how the nearing global spiritual and quantum economy is coming whether the world is prepared for it or not.

The Bottom Line

1. Saying "yes" to new ideas before they are evaluated is critical to forming Spiritual Transactions for the growth and success of organizations as well as contributing to individual global economies.

2. Risk should be seen as a part of investment, and a necessary part of the world.

3. Corporations are becoming part of the emerging global spiritual economy and serve citizens as well as customers.

9

SPIRITUAL
MACROECONOMICS

Thought, not money, is the real business capital.

The spiritual is the parent of the practical.

—Harvey S. Firestone

—Thomas Carlyle

W hen considering this book's issues from a microe-
conomic perspective, it is easy to see the common
ground that exists between each individual. Spiritual
Transactions bring that common ground to the fore
to increase productivity and employee satisfaction. Taking more of
a bird's-eye view, it is time to consider what you can learn from these
patterns at a macroeconomic level.

Ubuntu

What does it mean to say that new countries are falling more naturally into spiritual economies because they are skipping directly
into the information age and bypassing the industrial revolution that
most developed countries required along the way? In a section of
the book *Selving: Linking Work to Spirituality*, author Thomas Ambrogi
shared a story about his journeys to South Africa during the 1960s:

> One of our most moving encounters in South Africa was a long visit with Beyers
> Naudé, a renowned Afrikaner pastor of the Dutch Reformed Church who was
> defrocked by his church in 1960 when, with a ringing prophetic voice from the
> pulpit, he announced his powerful conviction that Apartheid was a sin.

He founded the Christian Institute, which courageously led the resistance of the churches for more than a decade. He suffered an ugly ostracism from his Afrikaner peers, social and ecclesiastical, and endured long bouts of the strictest kind of banning by the South African Security Forces. When we met Beyers, he was in his early 80s, frail and beautiful and almost translucent, with the shining eyes of a seer. I asked him what has kept him going all these years, in those times when everything seemed hopeless or in check.

He replied that it was the beauty of the Black South African soul, the uncanny ability of Black South Africans to forgive, their unwillingness to call for vengeance under the lash of so much terrible suffering. And he traced this to the African value called "Ubuntu." In the long traditions of African tribal society, Ubuntu means that no one is ever fully human except in community with others. When I asked whether this was a value brought to South Africa by Christian missionaries, Beyers thought carefully and said: "No, it is an ancient, pre-Christian value deep in the African soul, a priceless gift that Africans have to teach us Christians, if only we could hear. And it is my greatest source of hope for the new South Africa."[1]

The concept of Ubuntu is similar to our idea of the Spiritual Transaction. The Spiritual Transaction is not something that humanity invented for itself—it is the natural state of human interaction. Although it has taken the development of extremely advanced physics and a new global economy for the Spiritual Transaction to become apparent again, it is indeed an ancient concept. It predates the material transaction and lies at the core of all human relationships. It is ironic that humankind needed to nearly crack the code that reveals all the laws of the universe for us to realize something so basic and simple.

From Networks to Networks of Networks: People and Computers

Let us return to the example of the 1999 Seattle riots—a citizen reaction to what was happening on a global scale. The Newtonian business practices of traditional industries began to conflict with the rising culture of quantum understanding. While the corporations or trade ministers were busy focusing on the material aspects of global trade, individuals were witnessing the social costs of this trade. What brought about this understanding? Many claim that the 1999 protests were so successful—and so sudden—because it was the first time the Internet was used to organize disparate activists from all over the world.

I saw this kind of effect as a member of the Evolutionary Leaders, a group of 38 people who have undertaken a project entitled "Call to Conscious Evolution: Our Moment of Choice," a petition for positive change orchestrated by using Internet technologies to build an electronic network. The petition then began to circulate through our networks and also the networks of our networks. In a few short weeks, the petition received more than 40,000 signatures. The combination of social and electronic networks combined into a Global Mesh, which drew thousands to our call.

Our petition and the 1999 Seattle riots represent the emergence of a network of networks—or a Universal Mesh—the foundations of which required Spiritual Transactions in order to work. The offer of a large protest could not be guaranteed in Seattle, but the promise was there. The demonstration's success relied entirely on the actions of the individuals, no matter what the organizers tried to do. The activists had to trust each other in order to make things work. It was the formation of a network of trust similar to the network that WTO was trying to create inside the meetings in Seattle just beyond the police lines. Yet these two networks could not connect, despite the good intentions of both, because neither group was practicing purely Spiritual Transactions.

The quantum organization outside did not know how to deal with such giant Newtonian megaliths. Instead of presenting their case to those in authority in a way that would inspire Spiritual Transactions between them, or by taking action through pursuing advanced education or entering the corporate workforce in order to change things from within, most of these people simply tried to force the corporations to see their point of view. There was a violent interaction between the quantum and Newtonian organizations, which created social destruction instead of constructive talks, even when the Newtonian organizations present at the WTO talks were largely discussing issues that would see them moving more and more toward quantum organization themselves.

The Seattle riots represent something similar to the concept of Ubuntu because most of these activists were in fact anarchists—people who believe there should be no synthetic order in the world, and that the natural state of the human race is one without hierarchy. However, the Seattle riots are an example of how a misunderstanding of the Spiritual Transaction delimits its potential.

Two of the major factors in the rise of the Spiritual Transaction can be found in the story from South Africa and the story from Seattle. A third of the way round the world and 40 years apart, these stories have two common themes: the struggle for survival and a merging of ideological boundaries. In both these cases, people felt as if they were under threat. In response to this threat, people reacted in a joint manner as the threat introduced an environment that encouraged cooperation.

Global Chaos Attracting Global Order

The world today is at great risk. Between the man-made threats of global warming and nuclear annihilation, we are subject to a risk level that is unique to our history. Events like the food riots of 2008 represent our Malthusian fears moving forward; the notion of running out of oil increases the level of risk; and terrorism brings the risk of war right to our doorsteps. As discussed earlier, the bigger the risk, the more attention we pay to it; a big enough risk attracts almost all of our attention. And as this attention becomes merited, the stress level decreases and the threat actually introduces a Spiritual Environment.

Think of how nations band together in war and how workers form unions when facing corporate abuse. When a threat is big enough, it attracts so much attention that we are unable to generate stress elsewhere, and the risk itself is so large that it absorbs any attention thrown at it, also reducing the stress. Thus, society comes to accept things like the Great Depression, even if it does not understand why.

These are naturally occurring Spiritual Environments; yet if we do not recognize them, then they will always slip away from us. Spiritual Environments appear to be very much a part of the human defense mechanism. As our reptilian fight or flight response fails, our brains suddenly switch to their intelligence centers. Many of the new threats we face are universal and not isolated to any one nation. All people pollute the air and this is bringing ruin to us all. Our nations each aim impressive armed forces at one another and keep the fear of total war ever present. But the tragedy of the commons is resetting our brains into spiritual mode. Though if the threat passes and we do not realize the space we are in, it is likely that we could simply fade away from the ever-present spiritual world.

Another trend that provokes the emergence of a natural Spiritual Environment is the shrinking space between our ideologies. The cultural representations of many of our philosophies have merged into one multicultural global society. As we have begun to recognize the common themes in the world and get to know other ways of thinking, this had opened a new creative space. The imagination now has many more things to incorporate and our belief systems are challenged by foreign ideas. This creates an environment where creativity is more encouraged to emerge, along with many other Spiritual Assets.

The Emergence of Our Global Spiritual Economy

Companies from all over the world are entering the marketplace with a fresh take on how to do business. This forces us to come face-to-face with new ideas and their results, which begins to affect our own ideas of how to do business. The more influences there are, the more likely it is that our natural brain patterns will naturally and forcibly emerge from their ruts in dealing with new experiences. It is harder for us to sustain our habits, which creates the brain activity that results in natural creativity.

This is the more sustainable part of our natural evolution toward a global spiritual marketplace. Cultural globalization only increases as the ability for individuals to travel or to migrate increases.

An individual's ability to travel and migrate is affected positively by improving standards of living. Travel and migration leads to increased creativity, which leads to Spiritual Transactions that lead to an improvement in the economy—thus leading to an improvement in the standard of living. Once people start moving about different regions of the world, cultural globalization becomes an economic engine unto itself. This is part of why cultural globalization has come hand in hand with our economic globalization.

Cultural globalization is different than economic globalization; the latter focuses on trade, while the former is about culture. Increased cultural globalization leads to increased Spiritual Transactions, which leads to further economic globalization. This is consistent with the history of recent decades. The Cold War and the global tensions prior to it halted the exchange of culture between people. Yet this exchange continued in the United States, where immigrants and travelers from the world over shared their stories.

The process has less to do with what you leave in other countries than it does with what you bring home. Tourism in developing countries may bring profits to the local economy, but it is the tourist returning to his or her home country who provides real cultural exchange. You return with a different idea about the world, which influences your level of creativity and helps you discover greater openness.

Cultural globalization will exist as long as people do not make the same mistakes they did during the last great era of globalization. Modern telecommunications and the media keep us informed about the world, providing fuel for our continued tolerance of one another. With the rest of the world just catching up to the West, the world is about to engage in a significant era of cultural exchange and interaction. Yet even though the Spiritual Environment is here for the foreseeable future, society still needs to take advantage of it in order to harness its potential. There are many other reasons for this new Spiritual Environment—some of which are fleeting. We must, therefore, practice the ideas in this book and other ideas like them if we are to capture the profit potential of the age.

The intensity of the social and philosophical change worldwide has led many to speak of today as the Postmodern Age. The word

"Postmodern" implies that there was a Modern Age, which (according to social scientists) the world is just now exiting as a global society. Historians use the term "Modern Age" to refer to the period that began at the end of the Middle Ages. The invention of the printing press, the ability for regular folk to eat more nutritious food, and a social revolution created the context of a new era in human civilization. People began to organize themselves differently, soon enough in the now centuries-old Newtonian fashion. Discussions of social context, philosophy, and new kinds of politics arose across the Western world. Eventually machines were developed, leading to the Industrial Revolution.

Proponents say that the introduction of advanced science, computers, and global markets are pushing humanity into a new era of civilization. One of the major pieces in the postmodern philosophy is that a person needs to break free of old organizational patterns controlled by overarching themes. Postmodernists see humans as crudely compartmentalized and forced into synthetic divisions that hinder our understanding. These were perhaps the first people to predict the quantum revolution in organizational methodology, which revealed that these old ways of organizing were based on faulty principles.

It seems that the Postmodern Age is bringing with it conditions that suit the rise of a global Spiritual Environment more and more. In addition to technology that promotes closer human ties, a postmodern understanding of the world reveals that you cannot treat the world as one big machine or as a neatly organized library of facts. Comprehension of the world requires you to think creatively, and new knowledge about the world encourages the creative parts of your mind. The true way in which your knowledge must be organized is similar to the way the mind is best organized, too—creatively and without harmful habit.

Corporate Profit Overflow in the Global Spiritual Economy

I have talked a lot about the global Spiritual Environment, but I want to take a moment to acknowledge how this trickles down to the level of the individual worker. Postmodern thinker Jacques Derrida linked these ideas to the idea of forgiveness, for instance, in his book *Paper Machine*. The concept of forgiveness in a Newtonian world is much like our obsolete vision of morality: an experience must be seen as entirely negative or entirely positive; to forgive must also be to forget.

But Derrida wrote that,

> It is right to remember always that to forgive is not to forget. On the contrary, forgiving requires the absolutely living memory of the ineradicable, beyond any work of mourning, reconciliation, or restoration, beyond any ecology of memory. Forgiveness is possible only in recalling, and even in reproducing, without mitigation, the wrong that has been done, what it is that has to be forgiven. If I only forgive what is forgivable or venial, the nonmortal sin, I am not doing anything that deserves the name of forgiveness. Whence the aporia: it is only the unforgivable that ever as to be forgiven.[2]

Spiritual Transactions allow you to deal with utterly conflicting ideas in a neutral fashion—critical to an ever-changing economic environment in which the truth can be illusory. One major issue that strikes me as relevant at this point is that of corporate profit overflow. The obvious example of the day is the matter of oil company profits. Oil companies rely on the availability (or unavailability) of nonrenewable resources. It is fairly clear, then, that these organizations will not exist in their current form forever. The shareholders of these companies are investing in a higher risk form of company—a company with a business plan that will one day be impossible to follow up—that often relies on the luck of its oil surveyors and the whims of the global market price.

So when an oil company goes into profit overflow, it must take into consideration the fact that its future profit margins cannot be guaranteed. In fact, the oil company must also consider that there is a chance that it may encounter unexpected losses in the near future. Therefore, with an oil company the question of what to do with profit overflow is crucial to its long-term existence. In the Newtonian organizational methodology, oil companies are best protected by hoarding the profits or pumping them back into the company. Modern thought sees each company as a machine that must take care of itself individually. However, the lessons of the Spiritual Economy lead one to start questioning this wisdom.

A company with a finite opportunity to make money is like the improvisational theater group on stage—it is in its interest (more than most) to maximize its investment. The Royal Dutch Shell Corporation learned this lesson about a decade ago, when angry consumers confronted them about their bad environmental record. The company executives realized the risk that their limited time to function as an energy company could be seriously hampered, and that it was in their best interests to develop community programs and use some of their profit overflow to engage in macro-level Spiritual Transactions.

The problem is that the higher the profits are, the more forgetful companies seem to become of these natural economic laws. With billions of dollars in profit overflow, the company appears to forget its role as a limited enterprise. The more profits there are to be had, the less likely that a company will remember to engage in Spiritual Transactions. The temporary potential for independence from the community it thrives within provides a strong temptation. However, this is the time that a company has its most important role in terms of Spiritual Transactions.

The oil company gains the freedom to make Spiritual Transactions that improve its ability to survive when the tides of fortune change. Spiritual Transactions create higher future profits, but the need for these transactions is clouded by the state of the company at that very moment. Long-term investment is best settled into macro-level Spiritual Transactions, but the greed that accompanies profit overflow hurts the long-term survival of the company—and the long-term likelihood of continued Spiritual Transactions.

Richard Coughlin, whom I cited earlier, wrote something else of interest that has to do with how a company best accesses its marketplace and consumers. Coughlin wrote that:

> Family members, friends, and associates, with their shared confidence, time, and experiences, have the best opportunity to shape each others' preferences.

Hierarchies within these relationships determine which of incompatible prefer-
ences prevail. Parents, in particular, have a strong incentive and ability to shape
the preferences of their children to modify their behavior in ways the parent deems
desirable. Because of their superior incentives and ability to shape preferences,
families, friends, and associates will prescribe a set of desired preferences broader
than that prescribed by society at large."[3]

Engaging in Spiritual Transactions with the community is a way of accessing these preference sets that few other tactics can provide. In order to manage future prospects, it is best if a company can help manage future consumer choices. This is the law of advertising, but the Spiritual Transaction is perhaps the best kind of long-term advertisement. Profit overflow allows companies to commit material wealth to these Spiritual Transactions with less concern over whether their promise will result in any return.

A CEO who has developed rules around this kind of community investment is chairman and CEO of Salesforce.com Marc Benioff. Benioff established a foundation called the Salesforce.com Foundation that encourages corporations to follow his "1/1/1" model. The first 1 represents the company giving 1 percent of profits back into the community; the second represents giving 1 percent of employee hours back into the community; and the third represents the company giving 1 percent of equity to the community. Benioff was quoted as saying, "In both good times and bad, people are always eager to hear about challenges to the status quo."[4] He uses the system with his own company. Since founding his company in 1999, Benioff managed to survive the dot-com bust and then build a company with a billion dollars in revenue and a workforce of more than 3,300 within 10 years.

Great (Global) Groups

All companies may eventually need enhanced creativity within their ranks in order to help the business develop a sustainable sales structure. The best way to ensure that such people will be available to a corporation is to use any current comfort it has to ensure its future through the making of Spiritual Transactions that encourage creativity. Authors Warren Bennis and Patricia Biederman cited this concern in their book, *Organizing Genius: The Secrets of Creative Collaboration*, stating:

> *The lessons of the ordinary are everywhere. Truly profound and original insights are to be found only in studying the exemplary. We must turn to Great Groups if we hope to begin to understand how that rarest of precious resources—genius—can be successfully combined with great effort to achieve results that enhance all our lives.*
>
> *The need to do so is urgent. The organizations of the future will increasingly depend on the creativity of their members to survive. And the leaders of those organizations will be those who find ways both to retain their talented and independent-minded staffs and to set them free to do their best, most imaginative work. Conventional wisdom about leadership and teams continues to glorify the leader at the expense of the group. Great Groups offer a new model in which the leader is an equal among Titans. In a truly creative collaboration, work is pleasure, and the only rules and procedures are those that advance the common cause.*
>
> *Psychologically and socially, Great Groups are very different from mundane ones. Great Groups rarely have morale problems. Intrinsically motivated, for the most part, the people in them are buoyed by the joy of problem solving. Focused on a fascinating project, they are oblivious to the nettles of working together in ordinary circumstances.*[5]

The authors' definition of the "Great Group" is yet something else that reflects the potential results of a Spiritual Environment. Many researchers have tried to study how these kinds of groups arise, but this book is one of the first to understand the results of these studies. In order for oil companies and other companies with profit overflow to guarantee the best possible return on that profit is to enact macro-level Spiritual Transactions.

Indeed, profit overflow distracts companies from the most profitable status they can have in the global Spiritual Economy. There are significant traps that can hold companies back in the same way the individual is held back. Every company is made up of people; its policies are the result of group thought. Even while transitioning all normal, contemporary actions into a more spiritual place, the biggest trick comes with the rarest of occurrences.

Profit overflow is just such an example of the rare occurrence. These rare occurrences in the individual's life or the company's history bring with them their own behavioral history that is often seen as outside of the regular business or behavior of the company. Rare occurrences are often overlooked when it comes to the transition to a spiritual workplace, because they are seen as special cases. The danger in this, however, comes both from losing productivity in the face of your greatest potential and from the fact that these rare periods can be a catalyst that sends your company tumbling back into a Newtonian mind-set.

The strength of your Spiritual Environment will vary on a case-by-case basis, but the surest way to weaken it is to accept the false belief that there are exceptions to the rule of practicing Spiritual Transactions. This creates a slippery slope that can cause significant damage to your efforts. Rare occurrences can also come in the form of quarterly losses or social tragedy. During times like these, the business leader and the individual can be expected to succeed more often than before with the confidence and camaraderie a Spiritual Environment instills in your group. Yet if you are not there to monitor the situation while things are falling apart, then you can quickly find yourself repeating old mistakes.

At the end of the day, I think the overall strategy in this case can be summed up quite simply with the old Boy Scout motto: Be Prepared. Rare occurrences, whether good or bad, also create stress if there is sudden undue attention given to the situation. Though a spiritual group may function better, it is not entirely self-sufficient. There must always be those who actively inspire the use of Spiritual Transactions, and the stronger the environment becomes, the more important these leaders will be to the group.

The Bottom Line

1. Although it has taken the development of extremely advanced physics and a new global economy for the Spiritual Transaction to make itself apparent again, it is an ancient concept that predates the material transaction and lies at the core of all human relationships.

2. The Internet is the emergence of a network of networks, or a Universal Mesh. The very foundations of this Mesh required Spiritual Transactions to work.

3. In a truly creative collaboration, work is pleasure, and the only rules and procedures are those that advance the common cause.

10

SPIRITUAL ETHICS AT WORK

If you look to lead, invest at least 40% of your time managing yourself – your ethics, character, principles, purpose, motivation, and conduct.

—Dee Hock

Open your arms to change, but don't let go of your values.

—Dalai Lama

In the late 1990s, American Airlines teamed with business advice author John Capozzi to publish a small book of business quotes taken from his book *If You Want the Rainbow, You Gotta Put Up With the Rain!* A smaller version of the work was distributed, in part as an advertisement for his book, but also to bring awareness to the initiatives of the Partnership for America's Future chaired at the time by General Colin Powell. The book was exactly that kind of synchronic partnership that I talked about earlier in the discussion on macro-level Spiritual Transaction—it brought in more sales for Capozzi while making an effort to support the specialized causes he believed in. One quote from that little book that seems to suit this part of our discussion came from Thomas Edison. Edison said that, "If we did all the things we are capable of doing, we would literally astound ourselves."[1]

It is amazing to me how many people through history have said similar things, but did not quite make it all the way to the end. To capture a line from the film, *The Secret*: "These were the greatest people in history."[2] Indeed, these men and women were astute at accessing their Spiritual Assets, though perhaps without knowing exactly how to capture the *process*. As I have discussed in this book, there are ways that people naturally arrive in these places of exponential growth. And now you know how to arrive at these places of exponential growth on purpose.

The figures that utilized the Spiritual Transaction so well come from every period in history. Plato once said that, "Human behavior flows from three main sources: desire, emotion, and knowledge."[3] However, it was Aristotle who first saw that just as our feelings affect our behavior, our behavior affects our feelings. This was the tenet of his book, *Nicomachean Ethics*, a text that has echoed through the minds of scholars since 350 BCE.

Aristotle sees habit and experience as the most important thing in labeling a man as well as his acts. Aristotle also believes that virtue comes from impulse—the impulse of reason. According to him, man can, over time, create patterns in behavior that change his impulses, but his impulses are not immediately alterable. This prescient idea of Aristotle's is in line with modern psychology, as it has also come to the conclusion that behavioral patterns are linked to mental pathways.[4]

Aristotle said that, "Excellence is an art won by training and habituation. We do not act rightly because we have virtue or excellence, but we rather have those because we have acted rightly. We are what we repeatedly do. Excellence, then, is not an act but a habit."[5] The Spiritual Environment is what Aristotle discovered through his discussion of ethics, though the explanation of it was less practical as well as linked to another place and time.

Leonardo da Vinci, whose ability to become a master painter, mechanic, architect, and engineer—from his own admission—came from his creation of a Spiritual Environment. Leonardo left thick notebooks filled with his beliefs, and among those notebooks he wrote:

I know that many will call this useless work, and they will be those of whom Demetrius declared that he took no more account of the wind that came out their mouth in words, than of that they expelled from their lower parts: men who desire nothing but material riches and are absolutely devoid of that of wisdom, which is the food and the only true riches of the mind. For so much more worthy as the soul is than the body. And often, when I see one of these men take this work in his hand, I wonder that he does not put it to his nose, like a monkey, or ask me if it is something good to eat.[6]

Thomas Edison, the Dalai Lama, and Isaac Newton

It is astounding that Thomas Edison and Leonardo da Vinci operated hundreds of years apart yet were both in tune with the same spirit. Edison had the reputation as one who embraced his mistakes rather than hid from them. He believed deeply in positive attitude, creativity, and—even before Einstein arrived—gave us yet another quote that illuminates our discussion of the Spiritual Asset of time: "The reason a lot of people do not recognize opportunity is because it usually goes around wearing overalls looking like hard work."[7]

Talk of virtue and compassion can detract from the economic value of Spiritual Transactions if they are incorporated too early in the process. There are other connotations that these words bring with them—like the aforementioned *morality*—words that are false and discredit that which is attached to them. The introduction of spiritual matters into a business discussion must be flexible and based on the terms that the business is comfortable with. Great personal material wealth the world over comes from the economic institutions that already support us—trade pacts, companies, government treasuries. Therefore, spirituality must be used to accent, not deconstruct, the business of the world.

The Spiritual Environment and the quantum organization can come quite naturally out of the Newtonian environment. As Sir Isaac Newton himself said, "If I have seen further [than others] it is by standing upon the shoulders of giants."[8] In approaching the Spiritual Environment, you must be certain to treat your predecessors and the postmodern world's ancestors with the same spiritual hand that they addressed their contemporaries. Quantum understanding is something that came from a long history, not something that just popped into your head.

The Root of Business Ethics

The matter of how the Spiritual Transaction is related to business ethics must be addressed. Ethics are different from morality, again, because they are quantitative arguments that revolve around decision-making systems rather than normative value judgments. In this way, ethics have already become a valuable part of economic environments the world over.

Authors Ben and Sylvia Selekman wrote of the role of ethics in business back in 1956, saying that:

> In a world divided, as ours is, into competitive social systems, we must of necessity turn to reason, logic, and rationalism as the major tools for the evaluation of moral systems by which free people prefer to live ... This measure of rational control, innate and inescapable, we are apt to take for granted. But major issues of social justice still remain. By what appeals to reason we can determine whether the very abundance created by capitalist industry is being equitably shared? What standards determine whether a particular rate of profit is justified, whether given prices are just, whether wages are fairly differentiated between the skills of workmen, whether advertising is truthful, whether workers are entitled to have pensions, vacation with pay, and minimum annual earnings provided as a fixed cost to business? These ethical issues remain, though they have constituted, since the beginnings of industrial society, the stuff of social and religious discussion.[9]

The authors' observations reveal the role of ethics as the structure on which people often cast their value judgments or ill-researched notions of "changing the world." After all, ethics also change over time—as mentioned previously, the ethical nature of slavery or serfdom has been altered significantly since ancient times. The ethical nature of Communism has also shifted, as society has now watched the Marxist experiments of Russia, Cuba, Northeast Africa, and China fail. Ethics are responsive to the world consciousness of how things should best work in respect to social costs.

In a 1961 study cited by Dr. Fred Cook in his 1966 book, *The Corrupted Land: The Social Morality of Modern America*, a significant portion of individuals believed in the statement, "whatever is good business is good ethics."[10] The ironic thing is that given the idea of the Spiritual Transaction, this statement is actually true. Yet, this is not what the respondents to the survey meant when giving their replies. Authors W.M. Hoffman, J. Kamm, R. Frederick, and E. Petry conjured another international image of the origin of ethics as they have been used in cross-cultural societies when they wrote that:

> A metaphysical understanding of reality, the existence of a divinely arranged world-order, underlie all of the basic assumptions that result in the principles of African land ethics ... reverence ... the inappropriateness of land ownership ... the prescription of rituals involving natural entities ... [and] the importance of not treating natural entities as "commodities,"... All of these have a common denominator: the belief in God or a Divine Creator sustaining all natural life, in turn giving rise to interconnectedness and kinship of all natural entities including human beings ... [While] Westerners ... view any encroachment upon their "right" to freedom of choice and absolute ownership of all property ... as an unnatural occurrence, an insult against their dignity.[11]

In this light, the ethics of basic business seem to reflect the wisdom of the Spiritual Transaction. The basis of the idea of the Spiritual Transaction reveals that people all hold the same basic Spiritual Assets inside of themselves; it is just that their access to them varies from individual to individual, based on how their lives have gone. It is therefore natural to begin to see the overall environment in which companies do business as a shared environment that is best taken care of through the Spiritual Transaction.

The Business of Ethics

I believe that in a Spiritual Environment, the good of the many necessarily comes from the good of the individual. Putting the individual in the spotlight through the Spiritual Transaction is in the best interests of the company. The Dalai Lama spoke of the universality of this view of ethics in his 1993 speech before the UN World

Conference on Human Rights. The Dalai Lama stated that although putting the group ahead of the individual might be "traditional" in some regions, that does not automatically make it the best possible policy. He believes that instead of a culture shared by all people in regions like Africa and Asia, the ideology that opposes putting the individual ahead of the group is only held by the predatory governments in power.

The Dalai Lama sees individual rights as necessary for a person to pursue the best interests of the group. He sees individual rights as the tool by which collective rights can be attained. Whereas Western thought may see individual rights as advancing the well-being of everybody by allowing them to have maximum impact on the economy and availability of services, the Dalai Lama advocates a more direct use of individual effort toward supporting the community. Through this, the Dalai Lama believes that Universalism can be implemented into Asian and other "collective first" philosophies. Economic or social advancement and freedoms, for the Dalai Lama, requires the political and civil freedoms guaranteed only by a Universalist approach to rights. What he is talking about is a Spiritual Transaction.[12]

Tibor Machman wrote something else in his book, *Commerce and Morality*, that takes our discussion of ethics a step further, where he stated that:

> *Ethics is the discipline concerned with what standards are to guide our choices in life. This field of concerns arises in response to the question that apparently all persons must ask, namely, "How should I conduct myself?" And business ethics is concerned with the implications of the best answer to that question for one distinct area of human social life, commerce. The basic assumptions of ethics are implicit in the slogan "Ought implies can." This means: (a) if Bob ought to our should do something, he is free to choose to do or not to do it; and (b) some standard of conduct is identifiable with regard to Bob and other persons and their ability to make the right choice. So the two basic assumptions underlying ethics are that we all possess free will and that some ethical theory or system can be found that will provide us with standards for making the best choices in our lives.[13]*

Under this definition, the principles of the Spiritual Transaction are the best possible flesh to add to the bones of modern business ethics. The tenets of ethics are only evident when placed in a context that reveals their wisdom. There is a lot of evidence that this context cannot be found in a Newtonian or traditional business economy. However, the coming spiritual economic environment seems to provide just such a context that allows the full functioning of the brilliance of our ethical systems.

The Bottom Line

1. There is little struggle within the virtuous person with reason and his or her direction toward the Good. This person experiences almost automatic virtuous reactions to situations as they arise and in his or her daily actions as well. The continent person generally follows his or her reason but an irrational part clouds the path, creating the potential for nonvirtuous actions.

2. The Spiritual Transaction allows those aspects of our reputation that help our spiritual efforts last. Virtuousness, compassion, and sympathy are all reputation builders.

3. The basis of the idea of the Spiritual Transaction reveals that people all hold the same basic Spiritual Assets inside of themselves; their access merely varies from one individual to the next based on his or her life experience. In addition, people must begin to see the overall environment in which companies do business as a shared environment that is best taken care of through the Spiritual Transaction.

11

THE SPIRITUAL ECONOMIC REVOLUTION

If you build that foundation, both the moral and the ethical foundation, as well as the business foundation, and the experience foundation, then the building won't crumble.

—Henry Kravis

You are not a human being in search of a spiritual experience. You are a spiritual being immersed in a human experience.

—Teilhard de Chardin

Greatest Assets Hidden

Even if you encounter the right stuff to make up your Spiritual Environment, if you do not understand the mechanics of it then you will not know what to do with it. The Spiritual Economy is coming and all individuals must prepare themselves for it. In support of this, John Dalla Costa wrote in his book, *The Ethical Imperative: Why Moral Leadership Is Good Business,* that:

When we workers accuse senior managers of making business decisions free of any moral reference point, we are pointing out not an anomaly in their position but something we share with them. Another lesson, one more difficult to learn, is that the already great and growing investment in the economic dimensions of human life are in many ways abnegating the very meaning derived from spirituality.

The compounding worries about protecting jobs and surviving economic upheaval have only intensified the selfishness that most religions castigate and all spirituality opposes. We draw much of our meaning and spiritual awe from nature, yet unrelenting economic expediency is devastating the natural environment. We draw identity, duty and moral worth from social interaction, yet accelerating economic competitiveness causes us to tolerate more and more poverty, inequality and injustice.[1]

The Newtonian business habits of companies and individuals not only destroy the productivity of their businesses, but also of any social advances society makes as a whole. It is no wonder that our nations are split down the middle ideologically. Our society and economy has been built on a contradictory foundation, leading individuals into unnatural categorizations. When people hear themselves called an American, or French, or Spanish, or Canadian, they often feel proud in the same way those on the other side of the political spectrum do. Yet we all define ourselves as working citizens in ways that are not mutually exclusive in the right context. Corporate citizenship emanates not from our individual obstacles, but from the fact that each of our individual obstacles exist within the same space. Our context is the same, but the problems in front of us draw too much of our attention and create too much stress.

One of the best ways out of this is to advocate the specialization of philanthropic efforts. Creating macro-level Spiritual Transactions is as important as the Spiritual Transaction is to you at the level of the individual. If you want evidence as to how this can help your standard of living and social advances, look no further than the Great Depression. Irving Michelman expressed in his book, *Business at Bay: Critics and Heretics of American Business*, that:

The automobile was the key to the great increase in jobs and payrolls. There were 23 million autos on the road in 1929 compared with 7 million in 1919. It was the most practical and dynamic expression of America's industrial genius, involving not only native inventive ability but also mass production and the new techniques of modern advertising, salesmanship and installment credit. They all combined miraculously to change the morality, the landscape and the habits of Americans. Henry Ford was the authentic business hero even though the novelists failed to take him on and everything he said or did, crackpot or sensible, was major news.[2]

Henry Ford raised the consciousness (and the average income) of the U.S. worker substantially and believed that the more you gave to the worker, the better the economy would become. Indeed, "Fordism" is also an example of the Spiritual Transaction at work. The theory was simple: the more your workers made, the more money they could spend—perhaps on your own product, like buying a car. It worked well and the economy boomed; however, the principles of what was going on were misunderstood. People greedily clung to the material results without maintaining the system. The Spiritual Environment was seen as a Newtonian engine instead of the rise of quantum business.

The United States lost everything it had earned in that Spiritual Environment, and it was not until President Roosevelt made his great spiritual promise to the country that success returned to our financial system. But the Keynesian economics that bolstered Roosevelt's Great Society were eventually forgotten, too, as the material results began to cast a shadow over the way in which they were gained. Society once again did not understand how this great wealth had come about.

The booming 1990s and computer industry are yet another example of an opportunity lost. With the introduction of our ability to enter a new level of Mesh and create networks of networks of individuals, society came closer than ever to being able to understand the forces that were improving the lives of people all around the world. But society became distracted by the stock market tickers that represented the growing retirement savings of millions of investors. These men and women did not yet understand what "magical" force had arrived.

The Spiritual Transaction was a major drive behind what analysts called consumer or investor confidence. But instead of putting trust in our society and each other, we let the market dictate how much we should engage in what we could not see as Spiritual Transactions. I believe that the market would never have gone so high if we had known, and the market would not have crashed. Placing hope and trust in the individuals and the companies rather than the share price and what it means to our bank accounts, would have created a better climate. This follows a basic tenet of investing, one ignored only by those who do not know enough about the market or are trying to manipulate it—trust the reality of a company and its daily business, not the value speculators put on it.

The potential openness of culture, that the technology that drove those companies higher represents, was something famously advocated by Minister Gilberto Gil—Brazil's Minister of Culture from 2003 to 2008. A famous musician before coming to power, Gil believed in what he called "hacker ethics," and something he referred to as "open culture." Minister Gil believed that true growth could only come from the commons—an open society where things are shared in a way similar to the writings of Tapscott and Williams. The result of Gil's work has put Brazil at the forefront of intellectual property reform issues.

Gil's efforts also led to the opening of more than 600 cultural hotspots, where Brazilians were provided with free computers and free software with the goal of spreading digital culture throughout the country. Gil saw the open-source practices of many software designers as groundbreaking, and wanted to incorporate the values of those practices into other parts of Brazilian life. During his tenure, Gil's efforts brought computer access to millions of Brazilians who would not have otherwise had access to such technology. The move has been lauded as one of the key elements of Brazil's push to become a global power. Talking about the importance of opening up our best ideas to the commons, Gil stated that "This isn't just my idea, or Brazil's idea … It's the idea of our time. The complexity of our times demands it."[3]

Life-Giving Spiritual Principles on the Job

Author and Professor Gilbert Fairholm wrote that:

> Popular culture celebrates the material and largely ignores the spirit. But competition and compassion need not be mutually exclusive. Indeed, for many people, the goal of work may ultimately be to more deeply become people of quality.

The biggest mistake of current leadership texts is that they confuse dedication, mission, and vision with spirituality. People are looking for significance in their work and the opportunity to use their minds and feelings in concert with the energizing life-giving principles within them.[4]

Fairholm sees the connection between spirituality and its outcomes. However, I do not believe that people confuse the two so much as they have simply been blinded by the system. This system is the same thing that led to Robert Starratt's observation in his book *The Drama of Leadership*, when he wrote that

Considerations about the postmodern sensibility of leaders will appear too soft for many. The macho attitudes towards leadership still abound: play hardball, crunch the enemy, don't show your trump cards, kindness is weakness, nice guys finish last ... Oddly enough, the transformation of Eastern Europe was accomplished by playwrights, university students and workers through non-violent rallies. Oddly enough, the international agenda is disarmament. Oddly enough, the environment is on everyone's mind these days. Oddly enough, the inside traders and government tough guys are going to jail; the corporate raiders are going bankrupt.

The boys in the back room who espouse these obsolete views of leadership are out of touch with reality. The price to pay for these illusions ... is terror, and the nineteenth and twentieth centuries have given us as much terror as we can take. We must be human if we are to survive. "Soft" works.[5]

Starratt was witness to the beginning of this spiritual revolution at the beginning of the 1990s, and if society is to sustain it, then it must recognize what is really going on. If the British had not recognized that machinery innovation was more than a local curiosity, we would not have had the Industrial Revolution. If James Hargreaves's "Spinning Jenny" used to spin cotton had been seen as "a lucky break," instead of the beginning of something major, we might all still be involved in cottage industries.

Good Night Newton

I do think that a revolution is taking place right now. While historians and philosophers argue over whether the Modern Age is now over, society is witnessing the quantum organization's rise.

The Newtonian model was the basis for the Industrial Revolution, and the new models of organization are finally moving us past this point.

I "grew up" in the Information Age. I spent my decades in the corporate world watching the business of computers and information technologies grow from one of nascent curiosity to a fully mature industry. I witnessed the impact that information technology had behind the scenes on the growth and dominance of the world's most powerful corporations. For example, when I was Vice President of Corporate Development for Encore Computer Corporation—a NASDAQ-listed supplier of parallel computing and mass storage systems—I became well aware of the significance of Walmart's enormous information technology infrastructure. In many respects, Walmart's current success is partially due to its design of an advanced company-wide IT system that controlled its inventory on a real-time basis. This was supported by its own satellite communications system installed in 1987. By uniting the different stores and suppliers in this manner, Walmart was able to establish full openness when it came to the movement of its merchandise. It is this kind of open system that men like Gilberto Gil believe will advance the human society and any organization within it just as effectively as Walmart's IT infrastructure advanced its global reach.

The Spiritual Revolution revolves around the changes we are making in our organizational systems and societies more than it does around the changes we are making in technology. It strives to benefit everyone, but it is those who catch on first who will reap the greatest initial rewards. The exact form of the Spiritual Revolution is yet to reveal itself to us, but cultural globalization and the spread of quantum business practices seem to be a part of that initial bud.

Isaac Newton's major work on the mechanics of the universe came to us in the 1680s. The Industrial Revolution originated about 80 years later in the 1760s. It should be no surprise to us that Albert Einstein's new ideas of how the world works arose in the 1910s; and about 80 years later during the 1990s, the world saw the beginnings of the new revolution. Yet the Industrial Revolution brought with it great horrors in terms of the human cost, largely because the results of what was going on and the mechanics of how the world was changing were ignored.

If society is to avoid these same mistakes—this "rare occurrence" in human history—it must be sure to understand the mechanics of this new revolution—what it means, how it can be used, and where it can go wrong. The Spiritual Revolution can be different from the Industrial Revolution because people are more conscious of the world around them. People must be sure to become more conscious of each other and what goes on in foreign lands. The reaction to these things needs to become more effective.

These are questions society must take to heart as the new revolution comes into play. The Spiritual Revolution offers great promise, but it has the potential to drive us apart if we do not understand it. It can result in war, as the Spiritual Environment of the early twentieth century did. It can result in greed, as the beginnings of it already did during the 1990s. The Spiritual Revolution does not refer to an awakening of the good in people, but to a new era in human organization and industry. Quantum workplaces can still function at a lower percentage of total productivity. It is the spiritual workplace that allows us to take advantage of the benefits of the Spiritual Revolution and to overcome the potential stress, distraction, and unhappiness that any new tier of excellence can bring.

The Bottom Line

1. Spirituality is the most glaring asset missing from so many of today's companies.
2. There is a connection between spirituality and its outcomes. It is less so that people confuse the two, and more so that most people have just been blinded by the system.

(continued)

(*continued*)

3. There is a revolution taking place right now, as we witness the rise of the quantum organization and leave Newtonian models behind. These winds of change can be referred to as the Spiritual Revolution. Cultural globalization and the spread of quantum understanding are as powerful as the spread of Newton's ideas in the seventeenth and eighteenth centuries—in the individual, the organization, the corporation, the national economy, and the global economy.

12

HARVESTING SPIRITUAL TRANSACTIONS, SEEDING SPIRITUAL ASSETS

We let folks know we're interested in them and that they're vital to us, cause they are.

—Sam Walton

I want you to be concerned about your next door neighbor. Do you know your next door neighbor?

—Mother Teresa

What Are My Spiritual Assets?

I have mentioned several times that there are more Spiritual Assets out there than I have listed and described throughout the book. Some examples of what I already discussed include Time, Curiosity, Attitude, Creativity, and Openness. In order to discover which of these might be lying deep inside of you, I suggest that you complete the following list of questions and record them. I myself have used these and other exercises throughout my career to stay in touch with my Spiritual Assets. This list has helped me to be a better worker, manager, and leader—in both the corporate world and the nonprofit world, from General Electric to Unity:

What are three of the important things in my life?

Example: My spouse, my career, and money.

What are two things that all three of these things have in common, perhaps in terms of what they represent to you? In other words, *why* are they important?

Example: They represent success and give me confidence.

What emotion or feeling do you associate with the two of these ideas?

Example: Excitement.

What attributes do you envision someone having whom is always embracing that emotion or feeling?

Example: Bravery, Courage, Spontaneity.

What is one thing that you believe encompasses all these attributes?

Example: Curiosity.

You can repeat this exercise with any number of things, people, or events that are important to you; they do not have to consist of the *most* important three. Use this exercise to discover all the ways the things that you desire are connected to your Spiritual Assets. The more you do it, the more you learn about how to access your own personal Spiritual Assets. There is not a specific, set formula to discover them. Everybody is different. Therefore, most of the exercises in this section are intended to be general enough for you to do on your own. They may lead down the shadowy caverns of your spiritual core. Why? The more you discover about your innermost being, the more you can understand and capitalize on your Spiritual Assets, and achieve greater success.

The next exercise is designed to help you create better thought patterns:

What are three things I do every day?

For each of these things, what is one way I have never tried to do this task before?

What do I feel inside when I consider doing these things?

Am I comfortable with the fact that I am feeling this way?

What do I envision when I visualize doing the task in that way from beginning to end?

The point of this exercise is to start thinking about any habitual patterns in which you behave. If you feel too anxious or uncomfortable about the three things you choose, try another three. It is best to answer the questionnaire a few times with different answers to see if some topics are easier for you to think about than others. The last stage is about visualizing exactly how such a new method would work, which will already start to shift around those brain patterns. It also boosts your confidence as to exactly what might happen.

The last step is to enact these changes at least once. The best use of this exercise is to choose three new things each time you decide to enact those changes, because the goal is not to just switch things to another pathway through the brain but to start breaking up the pathways. You do not always have to start with something difficult, because every path break in your mind will lead you to become more practiced and comfortable with the idea of breaking things down.

The next exercise helps with making affirmations:

What is something that I feel will go wrong in the future, or something I am concerned about that might not turn out as I had hoped?

If I were to believe that this experience will turn out the way I had hoped, what would I think instead?

This exercise is shorter than most. Once you have the answer to the second question, simply repeat that sentence out loud. Say it over and over again. Let the thought come to mind and the words come to your lips throughout the day. Try for once an hour; it can initially feel distracting to do this consistently. This is also a method of breaking down your brain patterns.

The next exercise is designed to help you approach your first conscious Spiritual Transaction:

What would be the best possible outcome for me from this conversation, or cooperative effort with the person on the other end?

Do these outcomes conflict, and if so, will I discuss these conflicts openly with the person?

Am I sensitive to that person's conflict, so as to do everything I can to ease it?

Am I actively seeking what I want from this transaction?

Do I praise the person for their participation as well as constructively deliver any misgivings I may have afterward?

This is a list that reflects the general steps within a Spiritual Transaction. The exact form of your Spiritual Transactions will develop over time, but keep these general notions in mind within any such transaction. Remember that a Spiritual Transaction is based on open communication and the containment of negative intentions. It is also about your getting as much as possible out of it because it is about giving the other person as much as possible. The "give to get" idea often invokes images of giving and then waiting. In reality, a smooth Spiritual Transaction shows little space between the two.

If you are concerned with whether you know you are ready to create a Spiritual Environment as a manager, try answering the following:

What do I want from my employees?

Do I have an idea of what each person can offer?

Have I ensured that my responsibility within my current organization will not be misconstrued as personal failure?

Have I seen a response from my staff in terms of my new behavior?

Am I prepared for my idea to be rejected?

As you can see, this exercise requires more of the leader than most of the individually related exercises. The first two questions stem from concepts that I have already gone over in the book. The third, however, is critical to the success of your organization. Remember that today's companies are mostly Newtonian organizations, and that your actions can be misconstrued before any material results are realized.

Just as a regular employee does, a manager might have to make the decision to leave the company if it does not allow him or her the opportunity to improve the workplace. This kind of oppression results in career stagnation, as well as an inability to access your own Spiritual Assets. There is no way for you to maximize your own potential in a strictly Newtonian organization, and you have to be careful that the backlash from the company does not hurt your reputation. Nothing in life occurs in big strides.

If you can answer this question to your satisfaction and you are ready to move forward, watch for the reaction from your staff. The reaction will not always be positive, because the natural suspicions of the Newtonian system are likely rampant in your office. But if people are starting to get used to your behavior, or are curious about it, then you are ready to go to the next step—because you will be connecting with something the employee has already internalized.

Lastly, your idea and the Spiritual Environment may be rejected by the staff at first. There is no guarantee that people will realize the higher levels of productivity and satisfaction that could become possible, or that they will care. It could take a while to coax your staff into this new Spiritual Environment; you may need to seek some new people in order to make it work. The results at the end of the day, however, are worth every minute you spend to accomplish your goal.

Gandhi said it well: "Be the change you want to see in the world." More important than any exercise, or anything you can do for your organization, is the fact that it all starts with you. The Spiritual Transaction and quantum business exist to give you more freedom and greater control over your life. If you focus on widening the palette you use to color in your life, everything else should come naturally. For the Spiritual Environment is indeed the most natural state that great business, economic expansion, and the most effective people in the world can operate within. You are one of those people whether you know it or not. Every step you take toward taking control of your Spiritual Assets is a step in the direction of success. No matter how far you go along this path, you and those around you will always find yourselves in a far better place.

The Bottom Line

1. A Spiritual Asset is something that is necessary for you to achieve the things you really desire in life—including your work—and typically something that can be hidden away. What are the Spiritual Assets of you, your organization, and your industry?

2. Spiritual Transactions are based on open communication and the containment of negative intentions.

3. Spiritual Environments are predominantly Newtonian organizations. While you are moving toward the new quantum organization, your actions can be misconstrued before the material results come to the fore. Time is on your side.

NOTES

CHAPTER 1: LEARN THE SECRETS OF THE NEW ECONOMY, ENSURE YOUR PLACE AT THE TOP

1. Don Tapscott and Anthony Williams, *Wikinomics: How Mass Collaboration Will Change Everything*, Expanded Ed. (New York: Portfolio, 2008), 7–9.
2. Ibid.
3. Sasha Issenberg, *The Sushi Economy: Globalization and the Making of a Modern Delicacy* (New York: Gotham Books, 2008), 121.
4. Richard Florida, *The Rise of the Creative Class* (Cambridge, MA: Basic Books, 2004), 244–245.
5. Ibid.
6. Paul Seabright, *The Company of Strangers: A Natural History of Economic Life* (Princeton, NJ: Princeton University Press, 2005), 165.
7. Concept developed by James Cummins in conjunction with Tom Zender.
8. Merck, "Merck Announces Voluntary Worldwide Withdrawal of VIOXX," news release, September 30, 2004, www.merck.com/newsroom/vioxx/pdf/vioxx_press_release_final.pdf (accessed September 23, 2009).
9. Isaac Asimov, *Asimov's Chronology of Science & Discovery* (New York: HarperCollins, 1994), 2–6.
10. Rolf Lundén, *Business and Religion in the American 1920s* (New York: Greenwood Press, 1988), 119.
11. Ibid.
12. Katharina Kretschmer, *Performance Evaluation of Foreign Subsidiaries* (Berlin: Wiesbaden, 2008), 65.

CHAPTER 2: CREATING MORE COMPETITIVE COMPANIES AND A HAPPIER YOU

1. Charlotte Shelton and John Darling, "The Learning Organization—From Theory to Practice: Using New Science Concepts to Create Learning Organizations," *The Learning Organization* 10 (2003):353.
2. Ibid., 358–389.
3. Tom Zender, "Spirit, Science & Business." Lecture, Unity of Tustin, Tustin, CA (July 30, 2001).
4. Michael Phelps, *No Limits: The Will to Succeed* (New York: Free Press, 2008), 115.

5. Ibid.
6. Ibid., vii.
7. Ibid., 5.
8. Tom Zender, "Spirit, Science & Business." Lecture, Unity of Tustin, Tustin, CA (July 30, 2001).
9. Jean-Paul Sartre, *Nausea*. Translated by Lloyd Alexander. 1938 (Reprint, New York: New Directions, 1969), 115.
10. Jeffrey Rothfeder, "Speed Kills," *Conde Nast Portfolio*, September 2008, 98.
11. Ibid.
12. Ibid.
13. Michael Ray, *The Highest Goal: The Secret that Sustains You at Every Moment* (San Francisco: Berrett-Koehler Publishers, 2004), xviii.
14. B. Moingeon and G. Soenen, *Corporate and Organizational Identities: Integrating Strategy, Marketing, Communication, and Organizational Perspectives* (London: Routledge, 2002), 109–110.
15. The concepts of Spiritual Transaction, Spiritual Assets, Spiritual Environment, and Quantum Executive were each developed by James Cummins in conjunction with Tom Zender.
16. Richard Reeves, "If Beethoven Had Been Subject to the EU Working Hours Limit He Wouldn't Have Got Further Than the Fourth Symphony." *The New Statesman*, May 30, 2005, 32.
17. Kevin Maney, *The Maverick and his Machine: Thomas Watson, Sr. and the Making of IBM* (New York: John Wiley & Sons, 2004), 129–130.
18. Ibid., 130.
19. Richard Florida, *The Rise of the Creative Class* (Cambridge, MA: Basic Books, 2004), 44.
20. Ibid., 88.
21. Ibid., 131.
22. Ibid., 320.

CHAPTER 3: SPIRITUALITY AND RELIGION: A WORKING PERSPECTIVE

1. K. Hikida and G. Parry, "Beyond Quantum Physics: An Interview with Researcher Gary Schwartz, Ph.D.," *Whole Life Times*, September 2000, 41.
2. Robert McKee, *Story* (New York: HarperCollins, 1997), 11.
3. Matthew Zender, "Leadership with Respect to Popular Culture: An Examination of Advice Literature for the Aspiring Executive in Business." Paper presented to California State University, 1996.
4. Monica Edwards, "Wired for God," *Orange County Register Accent Section*, April 8, 2001, 4.
5. Dan Baker, *What Happy People Know* (New York: St. Martin's Press, 2003), 80.

6. Ibid., 81.
7. Jack Copeland, *Artificial Intelligence: A Philosophical Introduction* (Malden, MA: Blackwell, 1993), 39.
8. John Huey, "Builders and Titans: Sam Walton," *Time*, December 7, 1998, www.time.com/time/time100/builder/profile/walton.html (accessed September 10, 2009).
9. D. Harmon and T. Jones, *Elementary Education: A Reference Handbook* (Santa Barbara, CA: ABC-CLIO, 2004), 164.
10. Mara Der Hovanesian, "Zen and the Art of Corporate Productivity," *Business Week*, July 28, 2003, www.businessweek.com/magazine/content/03_30/b3843076.htm (accessed September 23, 2009).
11. Sylvia K. Selekman and Benjamin M. Selekman, *Power and Morality in a Business Society* (New York: McGraw-Hill, 1956), 20.
12. Jerome Davis, *Business and the Church: A Symposium* (New York: Century, 1926), 51.

CHAPTER 4: SPIRITUAL ECONOMICS: COMPANY AND COMMUNITY

1. Robert Solomon, *A Better Way to Think about Business: How Personal Integrity Leads to Corporate Success* (New York: Oxford University Press, 1999), 106–107.
2. Harvey Mackay, "Compassion Means Acting on Sympathy," *Orange County Register*, May 10, 2008.
3. Michelle Conlin et al., "The Top Givers," *Business Week*, November 20, 2004. www.businessweek.com/magazine/content/04_48/b3910401.htm (accessed September 23, 2009).
4. Ibid.
5. Robert Smith, "Buffett Gift Sends $31 Billion to Gates Foundation," *All Things Considered*, National Public Radio, June 26, 2006.
6. Erika Chavez, "Irvine Man Finalist for $1.5 Million for Philanthropy," *Orange County Register*, September 14, 2008.
7. Earth 911, "Five Environmental Initiatives Remain in American Express Members Project," *earth911.org*, July 20, 2007, http://earth911.org/blog/2007/07/20/five-environmental-initiatives-remain-in-american-express-members-project/ (accessed September 27, 2008).
8. Richard Coughlin, *Morality, Rationality and Efficiency: New Perspectives on Socio-Economics* (Armonk, NY: ME Sharpe, 1991), 9.
9. Garrett Hardin, "The Tragedy of the Commons," in ed. Axel Hulsemeyer and Julian Schofield's *Introduction to International Relations: A Reader* (Boston: Pearson Publishing, 2004), 120.
10. Jean Drèze and Amartya Sen, *India: Development and Participation* (New York: Oxford University Press, 2002), 196.

11. John Bowman, "The Dark Side of Chocolate," interview with Carol Off, *In Depth*, CBC News, February 2007.
12. Mike Davis, *Planet of Slums* (New York: Verso, 2007), 104.
13. Lynda Adams-Chau, *The Professionals' Guide to Fund Raising, Corporate Giving, and Philanthropy: People Give to People* (New York: Quorum Books, 1988), 49.
14. Richard Florida, *Cities and the Creative Class* (London: Routledge, 2005), 116.

CHAPTER 5: BUILDING SPIRITUAL ASSETS

1. Randy Peyser, "Soul Currency: An Interview with Rev. Ernie Chu," *Awareness*, September/October 2008, 11.
2. Ibid., 11.
3. Ibid., 12.
4. This concept is derived largely from "Saturation" in J. Cummins's book *Waves Crash* (Baltimore: PublishAmerica, 2003), 205–208.
5. Charles Fillmore, *Prosperity* (Unity Village: Unity Books, 2007), 24.
6. Doug Fischer, "Devellano Took Wings to AA Meetings," *Windsor Star*, September 8, 2009.
7. Ibid.
8. Monte Enbysk, "Feng Shui: Seven Ways to Create Harmony with Your Office," *Microsoft Central*, 2004, http://sportsplexoperators.com/newsletters/jan-feb01.htm#create%20harmony (accessed September 29, 2008).

CHAPTER 6: THE BEGINNING OF SPIRITUAL LEADERSHIP

1. Tom Zender, "Spirit, Science & Business." Lecture, Unity of Tustin, Tustin, CA (July 30, 2001).
2. "Defining Leadership: An Interview with Alan Hassenfeld, Hassenfeld Family Initiatives," *Leaders Magazine*, vol. 32, no 2, 36.
3. Ibid.
4. William Saletan, "Food Apartheid," *Slate*, July 31, 2008, www.slate.com/id/2196397/ (accessed September 29, 2008).
5. Rose Edmonds, "Workers Are Happy with Their Jobs, Survey Finds," *USA Today*, Careers Section, December 4, 2002.
6. Donald J. Harrington, "What Is the Place of Spirituality in Business?" *Review of Business*, vol. 20, www.questia.com/googleScholar.qst?docId=5001501125 (accessed September 23, 2009).
7. Gilbert Fairholm, *Capturing the Heart of Leadership: Spirituality and Community in the New American Workplace* (Westport, CT: Praeger, 1998), 133.

8. M. Gabel and J. Walker, "Leadership by Design: How One Individual Can Change the World," *Readandinspire.com*, www.readyaiminspire.com/ Bucky_Fuller_Leadership_Principles.pdf. (pp. 3–4) (accessed on September 21, 2009).
9. David Ewalt, "Immelt's Four Rules for Fostering Innovation," *Information Week*, September 25, 2003, www.informationweek.com/news/showArticle .jhtml?articleID=15200356 (accessed September 21, 2009).
10. Erick Schonfeld, "GE Sees the Light By Learning to Manage Innovation: Jeffrey Immelt Is Remaking America's Flagship Industrial Corporation into a Technology and Marketing Powerhouse," *CNN Money*, July 1, 2004, http://money.cnn.com/magazines/business2/business2_archive/2004/07/ 01/374824/index.htm (accessed September 21, 2009).
11. Michelle Conlin, "Religion in the Workplace: The Growing Presence of Spirituality in Corporate America," *Business Week*, November 1, 1999, www.businessweek.com/1999/99_44/b3653001.htm (accessed September 23, 2009).
12. Robert Solomon, *A Better Way to Think about Business: How Personal Integrity Leads to Corporate Success* (New York: Oxford University Press, 1999), 3.
13. Paul Elkins, *The Living Economy: A New Economics in the Making* (London: Routledge, 1986), 7.

CHAPTER 7: A SPIRITUAL TOOLKIT AT WORK

1. American Sleep Apnea Association, www.sleepapnea.org/ (accessed September 30, 2008).
2. Trey Parker and Matt Stone, "Die, Hippy, Die," *South Park*, season 9, episode 127.
3. Concept developed by James Cummins in conjunction with Tom Zender.

CHAPTER 8: BUILDING SPIRITUAL TRANSACTIONS

1. Bill Tancer, *Click: Unexpected Insights for Business and Life* (New York: Hyperion, 2008), 103–104.
2. W. M. Hoffman, J. Kamm, R. Frederick, and E. Petry Jr., *Emerging Global Business Ethics* (New York: Quorum Books, 1994), 122.
3. J.D. Glover, *The Attack on Big Business* (Cambridge, MA: Harvard University Press, 1954), 334.
4. David Frisby and George Simmel, *The Philosophy of Money* (New York: Routledge, 2004), 245.
5. Kevin Danaher and Jason Mark, *Insurrection: Citizen Challenge to Corporate Power* (New York: Routledge, 2003), 285–286.

CHAPTER 9: SPIRITUAL MACROECONOMICS

1. Thomas Ambrogi, "Pilgrim Person on the Road," Selving: Linking Work to Spirituality, ed. by William Cleary (Milwaukee, WI: Marquette University Press, 2000), 56.
2. Jacques Derrida, Paper Machine trans. by Rachel Bowlby (Stanford, CA: Stanford University Press, 2005), 160.
3. Richard Coughlin, Morality, Rationality and Efficiency: New Perspectives on Socio-Economics (Armonk, NY: ME Sharpe, 1991), 47.
4. Jim Kerstetter, "Q&A: 10 questions with Salesforce's Marc Benioff," interview with Marc Benioff, CNET News—Business Tech, March 17, 2009, http://news.cnet.com/8301-1001_3-10198391-92.html (accessed September 23, 2009).
5. Warren Bennis and Patricia Ward Biederman, Organizing Genius: The Secrets of Creative Collaboration (New York: Perseus, 1997), 8–9.

CHAPTER 10: SPIRITUAL ETHICS AT WORK

1. John Capozzi, Excerpts From 'If You Want the Rainbow, You Gotta Put Up with the Rain (Fairfield, CT: JMC Industries, 1997), 35.
2. "The Secret Revealed," The Secret, DVD, directed by Drew Heriot (Melbourne, Australia: Prime Time Productions, 2006).
3. R. J. Emmerling, V. K. Shanwal, and M. K. Mandal, Emotional Intelligence: Theoretical and Cultural Perspectives (New York: Nova Science, 2008), 153.
4. James Cummins, 2006. Aristotle's Ethics. Paper presented to Concordia University.
5. C. A. MacDonagh, B. M. Cuzzone, and Jim Hassett, The Law Firm Associate's Guide to Personal Marketing and Selling Skills (Chicago: American Bar Association, 2007), 1.
6. Leonardo Da Vinci, The Da Vinci Notebooks (New York: Arcade Publishing, 2005), 34.
7. Danny Cox and John Hoover, Seize the Day: 7 Steps to Achieving the Extraordinary in an Ordinary World (Franklin Lakes, NJ: Career Press, 2002), 67.
8. R. M. Howard, Standing in the Shadow of Giants: Plagiarists, Authors, Collaborators (Stamford, CT: Ablex, 1999), xiv.
9. Sylvia K. Selekman and Benjamin M. Selekman, Power and Morality in a Business Society (New York: McGraw-Hill, 1956), 125.
10. Fred Cook, The Corrupted Land: The Social Morality of Modern America (New York: Macmillan, 1966), 74.
11. W. M. Hoffman, J. Kamm, R. Frederick, and E. Petry Jr., Emerging Global Business Ethics (New York: Quorum Books, 1994), 246.

12. Dalai Lama, "Speech given by his Holiness the Dalai Lama, at the United Nations World Conference on Human Rights, Vienna, Austria, June 15, 2993" in ed. R. Tremblay, J. Kelly, M. Lipson, and J. F. Mayer's *Understanding Human Rights: Origins, Currents, and Critiques* (Toronto: Thomas Nelson, 2008), 115–118.
13. Tibor Machman, *Commerce and Morality* (New York: Rowman & Littlefield, 1988), 1.

CHAPTER 11: THE SPIRITUAL ECONOMIC REVOLUTION

1. John Dalla Costa, *The Ethical Imperative: Why Moral Leadership Is Good Business* (New York: Perseus Books, 1998), 60.
2. Irving Michelman, *Business at Bay: Critics and Heretics of American Business* (New York: A.M. Kelley, 1969), 78.
3. Oliver Burkeman, "Minister of Counterculture," *The Guardian*, October 14, 2005, www.guardian.co.uk/music/2005/oct/14/brazil.popandrock (accessed September 26, 2009).
4. Gilbert Fairholm, *Capturing the Heart of Leadership: Spirituality and Community in the New American Workplace* (Westport, CT: Praeger, 1998), 118.
5. Robert Starratt, *The Drama of Leadership* (London: Falmer Press, 1993), 109.

REFERENCES

Adams-Chau, L. 1988. *The professionals' guide to fund raising, corporate giving, and philanthropy: People give to people*. New York: Quorum Books.

Allen, B. 2008. Dryland corn yield and water use affected by seeding rate and row configuration. Paper presented at the USDA Great Plains Soil Fertility Conference, June 4. www.ars.usda.gov/research/publications/publications.htm?seq_no_115=233386, (accessed February 12, 2009).

Ambrogi, T. 2000. Pilgrim person on the road. *Selving: Linking work to spirituality*, ed. by William Cleary. Milwaukee, WI: Marquette University Press.

American Sleep Apnea Association. www.sleepapnea.org/ (accessed September 30, 2008).

Asimov, I. 1994. *Asimov's chronology of science & discovery*. New York: HarperCollins.

Baker, D. 2003. *What happy people know*. New York: St. Martin's Press.

Bennis, W., and P. W. Biederman. 1997. *Organizing genius: The secrets of creative collaboration*. New York: Perseus.

Bowman, J. 2007. The dark side of chocolate. Interview with Carol Off, *In Depth*, CBC News, February.

Burkeman, O. 2005. Minister of counterculture. *The guardian*, October 14. www.guardian.co.uk/music/2005/oct/14/brazil.popandrock (accessed September 26, 2009).

Butterworth, E. 1993. *Spiritual economics*. Unity Village: Unity Books.

Capozzi, J. 1997. *Excerpts from "If you want the rainbow, you gotta put up with the rain."* Fairfield, CT: JMC Industries.

Chavez, E. 2008. Irvine man finalist for $1.5 million for philanthropy. *Orange County Register*, September 14.

CNN. 2005. Carlos Ghosn: Nissan's turnaround artist. *World Business*, June 6. http://edition.cnn.com/2005/BUSINESS/04/20/boardroom.ghosn/ (accessed October 21, 2009).

Collins, K. 2008. The role of biofuels and other factors in increasing farm and food prices. *Grocers Manufacturers Association* (June 19).

Conlin, M. 1999. Religion in the workplace: The growing presence of spirituality in corporate America. *Business Week*, November 1. www.businessweek.com/1999/99_44/b3653001.htm (accessed September 23, 2009).

Conlin, M. et al. 2004. The top givers. *Business Week*, November 20. www .businessweek.com/magazine/content/04_48/b3910401.htm (accessed September 23, 2009).

Cook, F. 1966. *The corrupted land: The social morality of modern America*. New York: Macmillan.

Copeland, J. 1993. *Artificial intelligence: A philosophical introduction*. Malden, MA: Blackwell.

Costa, J. D. 1998. *The ethical imperative: Why moral leadership is good business*. New York: Perseus.

Coughlin, R. 1991. *Morality, rationality and efficiency: New perspectives on socio-economics*. Armonk, NY: ME Sharpe.

Cox, D., and J. Hoover. 2002. *Seize the day: 7 steps to achieving the extraordinary in an ordinary world*. Franklin Lakes, NJ: Career Press.

Cummins, J. 2006. Aristotle's ethics. Paper presented to Concordia University.

———. 2003. *Waves crash*. Baltimore: PublishAmerica, 205–208.

Da Vinci, L. 2005. *The Da Vinci notebooks*. New York: Arcade.

Dalai Lama. Speech given by his Holiness the Dalai Lama, at the United Nations World Conference on Human Rights, Vienna, Austria, June 15, 1993. In *Understanding human rights: Origins, currents, and critiques*, ed. R. Tremblay, J. Kelly, M. Lipson, and J. F. Mayer, 115–118. Toronto: Thomas Nelson, 2008.

Danaher, K., and J. Mark. 2003. *Insurrection: Citizen challenge to corporate power*. New York: Routledge.

Davis, J. 1926. *Business and the church: A symposium*. New York: Century.

Davis, M. 2007. *Planet of slums*. New York: Verso.

Der Hovanesian, M. 2003. Zen and the art of corporate productivity. *Business Week*, July 28. www.businessweek.com/magazine/content/03_30/ b3843076.htm (accessed September 23, 2009).

Derrida, J. 2005. *Paper machine*, trans. by Rachel Bowlby. Stanford, CA: Stanford University Press.

Drèze, J., and A. Sen. 2002. *India: Development and participation*. New York: Oxford University Press.

Earth 911. Five environmental initiatives remain in American Express members project. *earth911.org*, July 20, 2007, http://earth911.org/blog/2007/07/ 20/five-environmental-initiatives-remain-in-american-express- members-project/. (accessed September 27, 2008).

Edmonds, R. 2002. Workers are happy with their jobs, survey finds. *USA Today*, Careers Section, December 4.

Edwards, M. 2001. Wired for God. *Orange County Register*, Accent Section, April 8.

Elkins, P. 1986. *The living economy: A new economics in the making*. London: Routledge.

Emmerling, R. J., V. K. Shanwal, and M. K. Mandal. 2008. *Emotional intelligence: Theoretical and cultural persectives*. New York: Nova Science.

Enbysk, M. 2004. Feng shui: Seven ways to create harmony with your office. *Microsoft Central*. http://sportsplexoperators.com/newsletters/jan-feb01.htm#create%20harmony (accessed September 29, 2008).

Ewalt, D. 2003. Immelt's four rules for fostering innovation. *Information Week*, September 25. www.informationweek.com/news/showArticle .jhtml?articleID=15200356, (accessed September 21, 2009).

Fairholm, G. 1998. *Capturing the heart of leadership: Spirituality and community in the new American workplace*. Westport, CT: Praeger.

Fillmore, C. 2007. *Prosperity*. Unity Village: Unity, 24.

Fischer, D. 2009. Devellano took Wings to AA Meetings. *Windsor Star*, September 8.

Florida, R. 2004. *The rise of the creative class*. Cambridge, MA: Basic.

———. 2005. *Cities and the creative class*. London: Routledge.

Food and Agricultural Organization. FAO Statistical Yearbook 2005-06. *fao.org*. www.fao.org/statistics/yearbook/vol_1_2/pdf/Na-mibia.pdf (accessed February 12, 2009).

Frisby, D., and G. Simmel. 2004. *The philosophy of money*. New York: Routledge.

Gabel, M., and J. Walker. Leadership by design: How one individual can change the world. *Readandinspire.com*. www.readyaiminspire.com/Bucky_Fuller_Leadership_Principles.pdf. (pp 3-4) (accessed on September 21, 2009).

Gladwell, M. 2002. *The tipping point*. New York: Back Bay/Little Brown.

Glover, J. D. 1954. *The attack on big business*. Cambridge, MA: Harvard University Press.

Grocer's Manufacturing Association. www.gmaonline.org/publicpolicy/docs/biofuels/CollinsJune08.pdf (accessed February 12, 2009).

Hardin, G. 2004. The tragedy of the commons. In *Introduction to international relations: A reader*, ed. Axel Hulsemeyer and Julian Schofield. Boston: Pearson.

Harmon, D., and T. Jones. 2004. *Elementary education: A reference handbook*. Santa Barbara, CA: ABC-CLIO.

Harrington, D. J. What is the place of spirituality in business? *Review of Business* 20. www.questia.com/googleScholar.qst?docId=5001501125 (accessed September 23, 2009).

Hikida, K., and G. Parry. 2000. Beyond quantum physics: An interview with researcher Gary Schwartz, Ph.D. *Whole Life Times*, September.

Hoffman, W. M., J. Kamm, R. Frederick, and E. Petry Jr. 1994. *Emerging global business ethics*. New York: Quorum Books.

Holmes, E. S. 1926. *The science of mind*. New York: R.M. McBride, 151.

Howard, R. M. 1999. *Standing in the shadow of giants: Plagiarists, authors, collaborators*. Stamford, CT: Ablex.

Huey, J. 1998. Builders and titans: Sam Walton. *Time Magazine*, December 7. www.time.com/time/time100/builder/profile/walton.html (accessed on September 10, 2009).

Issenberg, S. 2008. *The sushi economy: Globalization and the making of a modern delicacy*. New York: Gotham.

Kerstetter, J. 2009. Q&A: 10 questions with Salesforce's Marc Benioff. Interview with Marc Benioff, *CNET News—Business Tech*, March 17. http://news.cnet.com/8301-1001_3-10198391-92.html (accessed September 23, 2009).

Kretschmer, K. 2008. *Performance evaluation of foreign subsidiaries*. Berlin: Wiesbaden.

Leaders Magazine. 2009. Defining leadership: An interview with Alan Hassenfeld. *Hassenfeld Family Initiatives* 32, no. 2 (October): 36.

Lundén, R. 1988. *Business and religion in the American 1920s*. New York: Greenwood Press.

MacDonagh, C. A., B. M. Cuzzone, and J. Hassett. 2007. *The law firm associate's guide to personal marketing and selling skills*. Chicago: American Bar Association.

Machman, T. 1988. *Commerce and morality*. New York: Rowman & Littlefield.

Mackay, H. 2008. Compassion means acting on sympathy. *Orange County Register*, May 10.

Maney, K. 2004. *The Maverick and his machine: Thomas Watson, Sr. and the making of IBM*. New York: John Wiley & Sons.

McKee, R. 1997. *Story*. New York: HarperCollins.

Merck. Merck announces voluntary worldwide withdrawal of VIOXX. News release, September 30, 2004. www.merck.com/newsroom/vioxx/pdf/vioxx_press_release_final.pdf (accessed September 23, 2009).

Michelman, I. 1969. *Business at bay: Critics and heretics of American business*. New York: A.M. Kelley.

Moingeon, B., and G. Soenen. 2002. *Corporate and organizational identities: Integrating strategy, marketing, communication, and organizational perspectives*. London: Routledge.

Parker, T., and M. Stone. Die, hippy, die. *South Park*. Season 9, Episode 127.

Peyser, R. 2008. Soul currency: An interview with Rev. Ernie Chu. *Awareness Magazine*, September/October, 11.

Phelps, M.   2008. *No limits: The will to succeed*. New York: Free Press.

Ray, M.   2004. *The highest goal: The secret that sustains you at every moment*. San Francisco: Berrett-Koehler.

Reeves, R.   2005. If Beethoven had been subject to the EU working hours limit he wouldn't have got further than the Fourth Symphony. *The New Statesman*, May 30.

Rothfeder, J.   2008. Speed kills. *Conde Nast Portfolio*, September.

Runge, C. F., and B. Senauer. 2008. How ethanol fuels the food crisis. *Foreign Affairs*, May 28. www.foreignaffairs.org/20080528faupdate87376/c-ford-runge-benjamin-senauer/how-ethanol-fuels-the-food-crisis.html, (accessed February 12, 2009).

Saletan, W.   2008. Food apartheid. *Slate*, July 31. www.slate.com/id/2196397/ (accessed September 29, 2008).

Sartre, J.-P.   1938. *Nausea*. Translated by Lloyd Alexander. Reprint, New York: New Directions, 1969.

Schonfeld, E.   2004. GE sees the light by learning to manage innovation, Jeffrey Immelt is remaking America's flagship industrial corporation into a technology and marketing powerhouse. *CNN Money*, July 1. http://money.cnn.com/magazines/busi-ness2/business2_archive/2004/07/01/374824/index.htm (accessed September 21, 2009).

Seabright, P.   2005. *The company of strangers: A natural history of economic life*. Princeton, NJ: Princeton University Press.

The Secret (DVD). 2006. *The secret revealed*. Directed by Drew Heriot. Melbourne, Australia: Prime Time Productions.

Selekman, S. K., and B. M. Selekman. 1956. *Power and morality in a business society*. New York: McGraw-Hill.

Shelton, C., and J. Darling. 2003. The learning organization—From theory to practice: Using new science concepts to create learning organizations. *The Learning Organization* 10:353.

Smith, R.   2006. Buffett gift sends $31 million to Gates Foundation. *All Things Considered*, National Public Radio, June 26.

Solomon, R.   1999. *A better way to think about business: How personal integrity leads to corporate success*. New York: Oxford University Press.

Starratt, R.   1993. *The drama of leadership*. London: Falmer Press.

Tancer, B.   2008. *Click: Unexpected insights for business and life*. New York: Hyperion.

Tapscott, D., and A. Williams. 2008. *Wikinomics: How mass collaboration will change everything*. Expanded Ed. New York: Portfolio.

Winfrey, O.   2005. *The Oprah Winfrey Show*. Season 19, May 23.

World Food Programme. Countries: Bolivia. *wfp.org.* http://beta.wfp.org/countries/bolivia (accessed February 12, 2009).

———. Countries: Namibia. *wfp.org.* http://beta.wfp.org/countries/namibia (accessed February 12, 2009).

———. Special Nutritional Products. *wfp.org.* http://beta.wfp.org/nutrition/special-nutritional-products, (accessed February 12, 2009).

Zender, M. 1996. Leadership with respect to popular culture: An examination of advice literature for the aspiring executive in business. Paper presented to California State University.

Zender, T. 2001. *Spirit, science, and business.* Lecture, Unity of Tustin, Tustin, CA, July 30.

INDEX

and corporate citizenship,
84–86, 88–90, 93–96, 102,
196
and corporate giving, 90–93,
100–102
and corporate profits, 179–183
and cultural globalization, 178
and development of religious
thinking, 8, 9, 14
and dramatic improvisation,
161–164
and emotional reactions, 11
examples of, 9, 10
exercise for developing, 205,
206
giving before getting, 156, 157,
206
influence of on others, 72, 73
and innovation, 31
meaning of, 9, 14, 15, 25
and meditation, 153, 154. *See
also* Meditation
mistakes and forgiveness,
92, 93
and morality, 167–171
as most effective means
of doing business, 15
and networks, 70–74, 79, 80.
See also Power of Mesh
and philanthropic
specialization, 90–92, 196
and rare occurrences, 184
and relationship between
spirituality and business, 9,
10, 25
and saying yes to ideas,
161–164, 172
specialized, 96–101

spiritual versus non-spiritual
methods of handling business
situations, 12–14
and success, 207, 208
and work as spiritual experience,
139, 140
and world hunger, 98, 99
Spirituality
and belief in God, 64, 65
belief systems and values, 15
and business, relationship with,
18–25
and communion with others, 38
and consumer confidence, 6, 7
defining, 6
discovering, 19
importance of in business,
21, 81
importance of to individuals, 20
neurological effects of, 66–68
and outcomes, 199, 201
and religion, 8, 9, 14, 25, 62–65,
79, 130, 131, 170
resurgence of, 17, 18, 38
and ugly side of business, 21, 22
Starbucks, 152
Starratt, Robert, 199
Stress
and blame, 149
and creativity, 115
employees, 40–42, 49–52, 79,
80, 82, 129
and fear, 167
and letting go of problems,
145–147, 155
and meditation, 67. *See also*
Meditation
and perfectionism, 146, 147